# THE
# ABRAHAM
# LINCOLN
# BRIGADE

also by Don Lawson

*The Young People's History of
America's Wars Series*

The Colonial Wars
The American Revolution
The War of 1812
The United States in the Mexican War
The United States in the Civil War
The United States in the Indian Wars
The United States in the Spanish-American War
The United States in World War I
The United States in World War II
The United States in the Korean War
The United States in the Vietnam War

▼▼

FDR's New Deal
The Long March: *Red China Under Chairman Mao*
The Eagle and the Dragon: *The History of
U.S.-China Relations*

▼▼▼

# THE
# ABRAHAM
# LINCOLN
# BRIGADE

## AMERICANS FIGHTING
## FASCISM IN THE
## SPANISH CIVIL WAR

▲▲▲

# DON LAWSON

illustrated with photographs

**THOMAS Y. CROWELL**

**NEW YORK**

The author wishes to give special acknowledgment to two of his sources:
*American Commander in Spain: Robert Hale Merriman and the Abraham Lincoln Brigade*,
by Marion Merriman and Warren Lerude (Reno: University of Nevada Press, 1986,
for material used on pages 13, 14 (paragraphs 1 and 2), 15 (paragraphs 3 and 4), 16, 46 (paragraph 2),
47, 48, 49 (paragraphs 1 and 2), 82, 83, 129 (paragraphs 2 and 3),
and 130 (paragraph 1); and *The Passionate War*, by Peter Wyden (New York: Simon and Schuster, 1983).

Library of Congress Cataloging-in-Publication Data
Lawson, Don.
  The Abraham Lincoln Brigade : Americans fighting fascism in the
Spanish Civil War / by Don Lawson ; illustrated with photographs.
    p.   cm.
  Bibliography: p.
  Includes index.
  Summary: Discusses the causes and events of the Spanish Civil War, focusing on the American volunteers
of the Abraham Lincoln Battalion, the key battles in which they were involved, and their reasons for joining
in this early fight against fascism.
  ISBN 0-690-04697-9 : $     .  ISBN 0-690-04699-5 (lib. bdg.) : $
  1. Spain—History—Civil War. 1936–1939—Participation, American– Juvenile literature
2. Spain. Ejercito Popular de la Republica. Brigada Internacional, XV—Juvenile literature.
3. Americans—Spain—History—20th century—Juvenile literature.   [1. Spain—History—
Civil War, 1936–1939—Participation, American. 2. Americans—Spain—History—20th century.]   I.
Title.
DP269.47.U6L36   1989                                                88-20263
946.081—dc19                                                         CIP
                                                                     AC

## PHOTO CREDITS

Courtesy of Marion Merriman Wachtel and Warren Lerude,
originally published in *American Commander in Spain* (Reno: University of Nevada
Press, 1986), page 65 top;
Courtesy of Morton Prinz, page 65 bottom;
Associated Press/Wide World Photos, pages 66 top and bottom, 68 top, 130, 132 top;
Robert Capa, distributed by Magnum Photos, pages 67 top, 68 bottom, 129;
David Seymour, distributed by Magnum Photos, pages 67 bottom, 131 bottom;
Abraham Lincoln Brigade Archives, Brandeis University Library, page 131 top;
UPI/Bettmann Newsphotos, page 132 bottom.

Map by Pat Tobin

# CONTENTS

Photograph inserts follow pages 64 and 128

# FOREWORD

Today, the Civil War that was fought in Spain between 1936 and 1939 has been all but forgotten, even
by most of the Americans of my generation. Many of
today's young people have never even heard of it.

But when I was in college back in the late 1930s, the
Spanish Civil War was a great romantic cause. Several
of my friends and I used to spend endless hours talking
about going to Spain and joining the Loyalists in their
fight against the Fascist Rebels.

All of us were fierce pacifists in those days, and we
were convinced that the Spanish Civil War was the
prelude to World War II. Unless Spain's Fascist General Francisco Franco, who was being aided by the
German and Italian dictators Adolf Hitler and Benito
Mussolini, were defeated, Europe would be engulfed
by a total war against Nazi and Fascist oppression. And
inevitably, we agreed, the United States would be
dragged into such a war.

But in the end all that my friends and I did was sit around and talk about the Spanish Civil War—all of us, that is, except one. His name was Max Marek.

Max was a farm boy from the Dakotas (to this day I don't know which one). All of us were poor—the country was in the depths of the Great Depression— but Max was poorer than most. His family's farm had been almost literally blown away by the great dust storms of the thirties, and Max had hitchhiked out of the area until he reached the green, pastoral part of Iowa where our small liberal arts college was located.

Iowa farmers weren't much better off financially in those days than farmers in the Dust Bowl and other drought-stricken areas, but they could still plant and harvest crops. Max got a job as a hired hand on one of those Iowa farms, where he worked for two years. Then he enrolled in our college, where he managed to get a small scholarship and a twenty-dollar-a-month govern- ment grant from the National Youth Administration, which had just been started by President Franklin D. Roosevelt's New Deal. For his meals Max waited on tables and washed dishes at an off-campus eating place called The Grill. It was there that I met him.

Max was not an easy person to get to know. He was tall and somewhat stoop shouldered, and his dark, gaunt face always looked severe and unsmiling. It was some time before I realized that his drawn features were probably the result of boyhood malnutrition. Max was also extremely quiet and seemed to be ages older than any of us. (Actually he was a sophomore when I was a freshman and only three or four years older than I was.) Not many of us smoked, because we couldn't afford cigarettes, but smoking was one of Max's few indulgences. (We didn't know in those days that smoking could severely damage one's health.) He rolled his own cigarettes, however, from a sack of Bull Durham, which, as I recall, sold for five cents for two sacks, and the cigarette papers were free.

Most of our bull sessions were at The Grill, where we sat for hours over nickel cups of coffee. Whenever we got into international politics and the Spanish Civil War, Max either hurried through his work or neglected it and joined our group. He never said much, however. Mainly he just sat and listened and smoked his hand-rolled cigarettes.

After one such session everybody else drifted away, leaving Max and me alone at our table.

Finally I said, "What do you think, Max?"

"About what?" he asked.

"About the Civil War in Spain."

He sat quietly, the smoke from his cigarette drifting up around his dark face and squinted eyes. Finally he said, "I think we ought to go join up, all of us. Not only us but all the young guys in the country."

I was a little surprised by the force behind his words.

"But you've never said so," I said.

He ground out his cigarette. "Talk's cheap. Look, I gotta get back to work."

That day was really the beginning of my brief friendship with Max. Often during the rest of the year we made a point of waiting for each other after class so we could walk across campus together. And we saw each other almost daily at The Grill. After our bull sessions there I always stayed on so he and I could talk. He still didn't say much in front of the group, but alone with me he got so he spoke more freely. Gradually a real bond grew between us. But I was still a little surprised when he asked me for my home address before I left for summer vacation.

"Where'll you be?" I asked.

"I'll be right here, trying to earn a few bucks for next fall."

But Max didn't stay there. In the middle of the summer I had a letter from him all right; but it wasn't from Iowa—it was from Spain.

The letter was short. It didn't say how he had gotten to Spain. It did say that he and a number of other American volunteers had been formed into a single unit called the Abraham Lincoln Battalion. He also said they were undergoing infantry training at a place called Albacete.

I don't remember whether or not I answered Max's letter. Probably not. For one thing I didn't know exactly where to write. I do know that when I returned to school that fall, our discussions at The Grill about the Spanish Civil War were somewhat subdued. We all felt guilty sitting around and talking while Max had acted.

Nobody heard anything about Max until much later in the year. Then one day somebody was doing some research at the library and ran across a list, in *The New York Times*, of Abraham Lincoln Battalion members who had been killed in Spain. One of the names on the list was Max Marek. He had died in battle along the Jarama River.

By the time we graduated in 1939, the Spanish Civil War had ended, the Fascists had won, and World War II was about to begin in Europe. Two years later the United States was in the war and all the rest of us who had sat around that table at The Grill had either been drafted into the military services or volunteered. Those of us who did volunteer for World War II, however, never felt we were the first to do so. I know I didn't. That distinction went to Max Marek. He was our first volunteer, and it is to his memory that I dedicate this book.

—D.L.

# 1
▼▼

# OFF TO THE WAR

Beginning in the late 1930s the owners of army surplus stores in New York City's lower Manhattan were somewhat surprised at the sudden increase in their sales of personal military equipment. They were also curious about the small groups of young men who were buying this equipment. Occasionally one of the young men would volunteer the information that he and his friends were going on a camping trip. But when asked if they were going into the Catskills, the Adirondacks, or on up into Canada, the replies were vague.

Finally the store owners stopped asking questions. The United States was in the worst economic depression in its history, and the opportunity of making a few dollars from these quiet young men was too important to risk offending them.

Steadily, in the months that followed, the small groups of youthful customers continued to arrive in lower Manhattan. And they continued to make their purchases—flannel shirts and woolen trousers, leather boots, woolen blankets, winter hats, tents or shelter halves, fleece-lined gloves, sheepskin coats, canteens, and mess kits. When the surplus stores ran out of canteens and mess kits, the Boy Scout outfitting centers in uptown Manhattan's department stores were suddenly invaded by this eager band of equipment seekers.

Then, as suddenly and mysteriously as they had appeared, the groups of young men would disappear. Their disappearance always coincided with the departure of a passenger liner bound for Europe from the nearby Hudson River docks. But within a few weeks new groups of young men—always in small numbers— would appear and begin their rounds of the local army surplus stores.

Who were these young men?

Gradually rumors began to spread that they were American volunteers for the Civil War that had recently begun in Spain. When these rumors became more widespread, their youthful subjects became more circumspect than ever. They became totally secretive following the publication of newspaper reports that Samuel Davis McReynolds, chairman of the United States House of Representatives Foreign Affairs Committee, had asked the Department of Justice to apply the section of the criminal code providing for a $3,000 fine or a year in prison for Americans enlisting to fight

2

in a foreign war. Several Spanish Civil War veterans were actually threatened with arrest when they returned from Spain, but most were simply harassed—some so severely that they couldn't get jobs.

Eventually it became common knowledge that these young men were indeed volunteers bound for the Spanish Civil War. They reached New York by any means possible. Many hitchhiked. Some rode freight trains. A few banded together in their cities of origin, pooled their meager funds, and bought jalopies that somehow held together until they arrived in or near Manhattan.

The young men came from all over the United States. Many, if not most, of them were college students. Others were teachers, writers, lumberjacks, farmhands, cowboys, soda jerks, gas-station attendants, merchant seamen, clerks, automobile mechanics, or day laborers, and a number were chronically unemployed. They had one common goal: to get to Spain and fight to save Spanish democracy.

What had happened in Spain was fairly common knowledge. It had been related in detail in newspapers and over the radio, discussed by columnists, and shown in motion picture newsreels (television, of course, was not yet available).

In July of 1936 Spanish army units in Spanish Morocco and at army garrisons throughout Spain had revolted against the democratically elected government. Proclaiming a Fascist revolution, they had taken control of large portions of Spain, making General Francisco Franco their commander and proposed head of a new Fascist government. Fascism is an undemocratic form of government with a dictator controlling the nation's economy and way of life. Under Fascism no one is allowed to criticize the government or offer any opposition to the dictator. All daily life is regimented, and the country's foreign policy is often warlike. Racism is also often emphasized. An example was Nazi Germany's fierce antisemitism.

Franco's Rebels, or Nationalists, were battling the Loyalists, or Republicans, who were fighting to save the Republic of Spain. Supporting Franco's Fascists were German and Italian infantry troops as well as air-force personnel. Germany and Italy were also supplying the Franco forces with aircraft, war supplies, and money.

The only major nation aiding the Loyalists was the Soviet Union. In an effort to gain additional foreign support the Soviets had established the Committee to Save Democracy for Spain. This committee sought volunteers in France, Great Britain, and the United States who would be formed into International Brigades to fight against the Franco forces. Also active in recruitment in the United States was the Young Communist League, a division of the American Communist Party, whose activities were directed from Moscow.

Many U.S. government officials were suspicious of the Soviet Union's intervention in the Spanish Civil War. They thought the Soviets were mainly interested in world domination, and the attempt to gain control of Spain was a major step in that direction. Consequently, these U.S. officials were strongly opposed to the recruitment of American volunteers for the Spanish conflict, arguing that these men were also being recruited to join the Communist Party by the Comintern. The Comintern, or Communist International, was the organization formed by the Soviet Union to spread Communism throughout the world.

The truth of the matter was that a number of the American volunteers had already joined the Communist Party in the United States, and many others were sympathetic with its socialistic aims. These youths had joined the Communist Party or become so-called "fellow travelers" because of the severe economic conditions in the United States. (A fellow traveler is a nonmember who supports the cause of a party, chiefly the Communist Party. The term is translated from the Russian *popuchiki*.) As the economic depression deepened and fully a quarter of the nation's work force became unemployed, there began to be widespread talk of the apparent failure of the American capitalistic system. The Communists fed this unrest with suggestions for a revolution and the overthrow of the American government. Few of the young volunteers were quite that radical, but most were convinced that there was something wrong with the American economic system.

The election of Franklin D. Roosevelt as U.S. President in 1932, and his immediate measures for widespread relief and economic reform, quieted much of this revolutionary talk, but there were still many Communist sympathizers in the United States. Actually, Roosevelt himself was not wholly anti-Soviet. Many of his proposed legislative measures resembled those already under way in Russia's planned economy. And FDR went even a step further. In November of 1933 his administration recognized the Communist government of the Soviet Union for the first time since it had come to power following the Russian Revolution of 1917. One of Roosevelt's reasons for recognizing Russia was to increase trade between the two countries.

However, FDR was not in favor of any U.S. intervention in Spain. For one thing he knew that the American people would not support any such effort. After the bloodbath of World War I the mood of the American people had become strongly isolationist. Roosevelt was to make every effort to keep the United States neutral in all world conflicts right up to its entry into World War II. But FDR made no attempt to back Representative McReynolds' efforts to jail American volunteers for the Spanish Civil War. In fact several historians have observed that FDR secretly admired the young American volunteers.

Most of the volunteers traveled to Europe by passenger liner. (Regular transatlantic air travel, to say nothing of jet aircraft, were still in the distant future.) A few earned passage on freighters or took jobs as deckhands on cattle boats. Those who used the passenger liners traveled as third-class tourists. Some had enough money to pay their own fares, but most secured passage money from one of the Communist organizations in New York City. There were also a few stowaways, who hid wherever they could aboard ship and were fed during the voyage by other volunteers.

The first group of some ninety-eight volunteers sailed aboard the French liner S.S. *Normandie* on the day after Christmas, December 26, 1936. Later volunteers traveled on such ships as the Holland America Line's S.S. *Rotterdam*, the United States liner S.S. *Washington*, and several others. The immediate destination for most volunteers was the French port of Le Havre, but a few landed in Holland or Belgium.

As soon as they went ashore, they contacted one of the local Communist committees, whose members provided a few francs for railroad fare to the Spanish border and usually a guide. During the few days the volunteers spent in France, they tried to pass themselves off as student tourists, but they fooled few people. Nevertheless, the French, who were generally sympathetic with the Spanish Loyalists, went along with the deception. France was still a neutral country, and consequently could not openly aid either side in the conflict.

An overnight train ride took the volunteers to Perpignan or one of the other towns and cities at the foot of the Pyrenees, the mountain range that served as a gateway into the Spanish province of Catalonia. Early the next morning they crossed the French border and started on up into the Pyrenees. Those volunteers who were lucky were transported by buses on this leg of their journey. Many others had to walk, and the seven- or eight-hour hike was a grueling one.

Whether they rode or walked, all the volunteers eventually wound up at the Spanish town of Figueras in Catalonia. Before the war ended, some 3,000 young Americans would arrive in Spain in this way and at this particular town.

From Figueras, where the Americans in their U.S. Army surplus-store uniforms marched through town and were cheered by the Catalonians, the war-bound warriors boarded a succession of slow-moving trains and traveled down along the Spanish coast. Again they paraded and were cheered in Barcelona and Valencia, where the people shared with them some of their meager supplies of food.

Finally, the week-long trip down across Spain took the young American volunteers into the town of Albacete. This was the headquarters of the International Brigades. It was here that the Abraham Lincoln Battalion came into being, and it was from here that it first went into battle against Franco's Fascists.

# 2

## SCHOOL OF THE SOLDIER

It is not known who first suggested the name Abraham Lincoln Battalion for the American volunteers fighting in Spain. It is known that once it was suggested, all the Americans then present voted in favor of it. Later there was also a George Washington Battalion, but after a brief time it was absorbed by the Abraham Lincoln Battalion—or the Lincolns, as its members were more generally called. Although the American unit was officially the Abraham Lincoln Battalion of the XV International Brigade, it soon gained unofficial status as the Abraham Lincoln Brigade through popular usage.

As soon as they arrived at their training base, the American volunteers, like all rookie soldiers before them, were informally enrolled in what is commonly called the School of the Soldier. They arose at dawn and, after roll call and a quick breakfast of coffee, bread, and perhaps meat and fresh fruit, began a day of close-order drill (marching in cadence), advancing as skirmishers, or in loose formation, across open fields, and taking cover in nearby underbrush. They also learned how to strip or take apart and clean rifle-bolt assemblies and machine-gun firing mechanisms and, later, how to fire them.

The first rifles they received were World War I relics, Canadian Rosses, British Enfields, and an occasional American Springfield. All were thick with Cosmoline, a petroleum grease, and many were still in their original packing cases. The men spent hours cleaning their rifles and getting them in shape to fire. Cleaning rags were at a premium, and sometimes the men used pieces of their own shirts or underwear for this purpose.

Ammunition, hand grenades, and mortars and mortar shells were extremely scarce, so actual time on the firing range was limited to a few hours a day with no more than five shots per man being allowed on any given day. Not infrequently the men fired a few rounds into nearby bluffs or hills just to see if their weapons were working. This shortage of first-class equipment and ammunition was to plague not just the Lincolns but all the Loyalists throughout the war. Sometimes boxes of assorted kinds of ammunition would be made available, and the men would have to root through them to find rounds that would fit their rifles.

Gas masks were also issued, since gas had been used by both sides in World War I and was expected to be used in this one. (As it turned out, it was not.) The

World War I masks, however, were uncomfortable to wear and awkward to carry and soon began to be discarded. In actual combat, when the men began to strip down their field packs and other gear in order to be able to move quickly under fire, the gas masks were among the first to go.

Some of the trainees also began to replace their army-surplus clothes with dark-blue coveralls, and a few began to wear the popular berets. The coveralls were supplied by the Spanish people and were comfortable to wear. They also served as a kind of uniform. Many of the men replaced their leather shoes with the hemp-soled Spanish sandals called *alpargatas* or *espadrilles*. The handful of American officers could have passed for World War I officers in their breeches, their leather leggings or puttees, their blouselike jackets, and the Sam Brown belts with revolvers at their sides. Sam Brown belts were worn around the waist and over the shoulder, somewhat like safety belts in today's automobiles.

After the day's training the men ate their evening meals, which were as monotonously the same as those eaten in the field at noon—*garbanzos* (Spanish beans or chick peas) or rice mixed with some kind of unidentified and unidentifiable meat, which the soldiers called burro meat; dry bread; coffee; and perhaps oranges. Two things most men craved were sugar, or anything sweet, and cigarettes. Bartering went on constantly among them and with the Spanish civilians for these scarce items. Each man was usually issued twenty Gauloise cigarettes a week, and often one cigarette was shared by up to fifteen men.

Nevertheless, morale among these early members of the Lincoln Brigade was remarkably high. They were, first of all, volunteers in what they considered to be a noble cause, and in these first days there was a great spirit of adventure among them. Secondly, poverty and scarcities were no novelties for men who had just come from the depression-ridden United States. Finally, the Spanish people themselves did much to raise the volunteers' spirits. Poverty-stricken themselves, the Spanish peasants nevertheless did everything in their power to make these foreign youths in their midst feel welcome. There was, of course, the initial barrier of language, but soon the Americans were learning a kind of pidgin Spanish and the Spanish a kind of pidgin English. Early encounters began with attempts at barter, and these exchanges frequently grew into deep friendships. What the Spanish peasants had, which was little enough, was shared with their comrades from overseas. Sometimes this was only a handful of scallions pulled from a field. Occasionally it was a few spoonfuls of marmalade. Less frequently it was tobacco or a bottle of wine. And the Americans in turn gave to their new Spanish friends whatever they themselves had available.

One of the men who helped train the first Lincolns was an American. His name was Robert Merriman.

Captain Merriman would also lead them in their first battles.

Robert Hale Merriman was in his late twenties when he enlisted to fight in Spain. Most of the other members of the Lincoln Brigade were still in their late teens or early twenties. Merriman had grown up in California. His father had been a West Coast lumberjack and his mother had been modestly successful writing popular fiction. The family was poor, however, and young Bob had worked all through his teens as a logger and part-time janitor. Nevertheless, he made excellent grades all through Santa Cruz High School and was awarded a scholarship at the University of Nevada.

Six feet two inches tall and weighing one hundred ninety pounds, Bob was an ideal candidate for the Nevada University football team, on which he played until he hurt his back. He also joined the Reserve Officers Training Corps (ROTC), not because he was especially interested in the military but because it paid $8.50 a month. In addition, he worked part-time as a ranch hand to help pay his way through school. Despite all his extracurricular activities Bob was a straight-A student.

At a dance near Reno in the fall of 1928, just before the start of his freshman year, young Merriman met Marion Stone. Marion, who was also a freshman that year, had grown up in Reno. She too had to work her way through school. The two fell in love and were sweethearts all through college. They were married on

13

their graduation day in 1932. Then, in an old jalopy, they drove to California, where Bob had a graduate-school scholarship to study economics at the University of California at Berkeley.

Marion later said it wasn't until some time after they were married that she realized what an extreme political liberal her husband was. "Bob was a political idealist," she said. "He never made a formal commitment to the Communist Party, but he was a leftist who believed in taking action to support one's liberal beliefs." Marion herself was more conservative, but gradually she came to share her husband's political views.

At Berkeley Merriman continued to be a straight-A student. He also became keenly interested in the radical experiment in government being carried on in the Soviet Union. Many students and their teachers at this time thought that the Russians were creating a utopian society in which such evils as economic depression would be eliminated. Under Communism—or Marxist-Leninist socialism, as the Russians called it—there would be no classes of society with special privileges. All people would cooperate freely, and each person would be paid not according to his or her work, but according to his or her need.

It would be many years—not until after World War II, in fact—before the free world fully realized that Soviet Communism had actually created a form of ruthless dictatorship. During the very same period that Soviet dictator Joseph Stalin was supporting the Republican government in Spain, he was carrying out a series of purges in his own country that resulted in the deaths of thousands of Russian men and women. Stalin later said these purges were necessary to eliminate people who were "plotting against the state."

But in Merriman's college days the Soviet experiment in government was greatly admired by many young American political idealists, and it was fashionable for students, teachers, and journalists to visit the Soviet Union to see the noble experiment in action. One famous writer and editor, Lincoln Steffens, visited Russia and upon his return proclaimed: "I have seen the future, and it works."

Merriman was among those who wanted to see the Soviet Union at close range. After two years of graduate study he obtained a $900-a-year fellowship from the University of California to study the economics of rural agriculture in Russia. He and his wife were to be based in Moscow. They left for the Soviet Union in January of 1935.

The Merrimans had not been in the Soviet Union long when news of the Spanish political turmoil began to be discussed among their Russian friends. When the Civil War began in Spain the following year, stories about it began to appear on the front pages of Russian newspapers. By the autumn of 1936 Marion noticed that her husband had become more and more preoccupied with accounts of the foreign volunteers who were going to Spain to fight along with the Republican

Loyalists against Franco's Fascists. One day he suddenly said to her, "I think I'm going to die with my boots on." She knew then that he was seriously considering becoming a volunteer.

Marion tried to talk her husband out of such a decision. She pointed out that he would be of much more value living and working for what he believed in than foolishly dying for it. But he seemed not to be listening.

A few weeks later Merriman came home and told his wife he had just heard that the first American volunteers for the Spanish Civil War had arrived in Spain.

"I'm going too," he said.

All that night Marion tried to argue him out of his decision, but Merriman was adamant. He pointed out that the Americans would need training, training that he could help give them. He reminded her of his ROTC experience and the fact that he had been commissioned a second lieutenant upon his graduation from the University of Nevada. But most important, Merriman said flatly, was the fact that he felt morally committed to put his life where his mouth had been.

When Merriman left for Paris and Spain, Marion remained behind in Moscow. But it would not be long before she joined him. At this time neither of the Merrimans could possibly have foreseen that he would become the first commander of the Abraham Lincoln Brigade in battle, and that she would become its only woman member. In addition, and equally unforeseeable, was the fact that Ernest Hemingway would model

Robert Jordan, the hero of his best-selling novel *For Whom the Bell Tolls*, after Robert Merriman. The novel, which would help Hemingway win the Nobel prize for literature in 1954, would later be made into an award-winning motion picture starring Gary Cooper and Ingrid Bergman.

After Merriman arrived in Paris, he made his way down into Spain and to Albacete. There, on January 22, 1937, he joined the thousands of volunteers from some fifty-four countries who were forming the International Brigades. Many of the volunteers, he observed, were simply political idealists like himself, but most seemed to be Communists recruited by the Soviet Union's Comintern.

As soon as it was learned that Merriman was a second lieutenant, he was interviewed by the base commander, General André Marty. Marty was a big bear of a Frenchman who wore an enormous black beret that hung down to his shoulders. He had a huge walrus mustache and a thunderous voice, which he liked to use. He used it now on Merriman, telling him that the Americans were the most undisciplined of the volunteers and that if they didn't shape up he was going to send them all home. Then he told Merriman it would be his job to turn the undisciplined rabble of Americans into soldiers ready for combat.

Merriman was not much impressed with General Marty, and he later learned that not many other knowledgeable people were either. Ilya Ehrenburg, a highly

17

regarded Soviet journalist, said Marty was a "mentally sick man." Hemingway, who was a correspondent for American newspapers during much of the war, called Marty a "swine" for having several International Brigaders executed for insubordination. Marty later admitted to having at least five hundred men shot during the course of the war for alleged espionage. He insisted that certain Loyalists were guilty of reporting his military plans to Franco's forces. Eventually Marty was expelled from the Communist Party, but at the start of the Spanish Civil War he was a great favorite among Moscow officials for his heroic role in the Russian Revolution of 1917. Although French, Marty believed in the Soviet Communists' goal of worldwide revolution.

If Merriman was not impressed with Marty, he was impressed by the obvious need for instilling discipline into his American charges. The best way to do this, he decided, was through rigorous training.

The men took to Merriman almost immediately, more than they had taken to their earlier commander, James Harris. Harris was supposed to have had some military experience serving as a sergeant with the U.S. armed forces in China, but if this was true it had not been evident to the recruits. His orders had been unclear and contradictory, and soon the men had virtually ignored him.

Merriman, on the other hand, showed strong leadership qualities. As more and more Americans arrived—

by now the original ninety-six had swelled to more than four hundred—Merriman organized them into separate small units (squads and platoons), and he and Marty's aides lectured them on trench warfare, the use of grenades and small weapons, signaling, scouting and patrolling, and map and compass reading. Since Merriman seemed to know what he was talking about, the men rallied to him.

Merriman also emphasized the importance of traditional military authority. This meant accepting the decisions passed down through the chain of command from general to private. It also meant showing respect at all times to one's superiors in rank and promptly carrying out the orders from those superiors.

Getting his men to understand and accept the traditional concept of military authority, Merriman knew, would be no easy task. Free and independent Americans were not used to being bluntly told what to do, and the members of the Abraham Lincoln Brigade were even more free and independent than most Americans. The same could be said of all the members of the International Brigades.

When the International Brigades had first begun to form, the volunteers favored total democracy in their military organization. Officers and noncommissioned officers (corporals and sergeants) were to be selected only after they had proven their merit in combat. Since all the men were volunteers and thus "equals," there was to be no right of authority by one rank over another. These and other militarily impossible arrangements—voting on whether or not to follow orders, for example—had resulted in sheer chaos. Since then the men had been slowly weaned away from their naive ideas, but Merriman realized there was still much work to do.

To accomplish his goal Merriman did not hesitate to adopt Communist training methods. When the Spanish government had first come under attack by the Fascist Rebels, it was the highly disciplined Communist Party that had forged the first army to fight against the rebelling generals. The Party was directed by the Comintern officials from Moscow then, and the army was still being directed from there. Merriman knew this. His decision to go along with Communist training methods was not a political but a military decision, however. He believed the Communists' disciplined techniques offered the best way to fight Franco and, indirectly, Hitler and Mussolini.

As a result of his decision, Merriman added an officer to his staff who filled a role unlike that in any American or British military organization of that time. This was the battalion *commissar*, a unique Communist Party functionary attached to all military units. The original commissar of the Abraham Lincoln Brigade was a man named Samuel Stember.

The job of the commissar was to serve as a combination morale officer and political teacher. Since this was indeed a volunteer army, Merriman agreed that the soldiers were not expected to follow orders blindly. They were, however, expected to follow orders. But they would probably do what they were told only if they fully understood why these orders were important and how they supported the cause for which they were fighting.

Also, just because they were here as volunteer fighters for freedom, did not necessarily mean that they fully understood the fundamental causes of the war. The job of the commissar was to give them what amounted to a survey course in Spanish history and an explanation of circumstances that had led to the present Civil War. If that meant their getting a certain amount of political indoctrination along the way, then, Merriman felt, so be it. He would leave it up to their own judgment to decide on the merits of Communist doctrine. And since many of the men were already Communists or Communist sympathizers, the commissar's political message would not come as any surprise to them.

Consequently, when Commissar Stember gave his first lectures on Spanish history, Commander Merriman ordered all his men to attend. And Merriman set an example by being one of the most attentive members of Stember's audience.

# 3

▼▼

# BACKGROUND FOR WAR

Spain, Commissar Stember pointed out, had reached its glory days in the late fifteenth century, when it was known throughout Europe as "the mistress of the world." Not only had Spain's King Ferdinand and Queen Isabella financed the voyage on which Columbus discovered America, but they had also supported Spanish explorers who laid claim to the areas of present-day Mexico, Central America, much of South America, Cuba, Jamaica, the Dominican Republic, California, New Mexico, and Texas. In the sixteenth century Spain added parts of North Africa to its conquests, as well as the Philippine Islands, Portugal, and the Canary Islands and Balearic Islands.

But Spain's day in the sun had been relatively brief. In the late sixteenth century Philip II, then the King of Spain, attempted to conquer England. However, Philip's great Spanish Armada (fleet) of some 130 warships was virtually wiped out by the English war fleet in the English Channel in late July and early August of 1588. The victorious British fleet was led by Sir Francis Drake. Many of the Spanish vessels that did manage to escape the British were destroyed by storms on their way home. It is estimated that only about 60 of the original vessels in the Spanish Armada got back to Spain. After this defeat Spain lost most of its prestige, prestige that it has never really regained to the present day.

During the next several centuries Spain was almost constantly at war in Europe in an attempt to reestablish itself as a world power. During the American Revolution Spain joined with France in aiding the colonists against Great Britain, but in 1782 it seized Florida, which it held until the United States purchased it in 1819.

Early in the nineteenth century Spain tried once again to defeat Great Britain. This time it joined its war fleet with that of France. The combined Spanish and French fleets met the British off Cape Trafalgar along the southern coast of Spain near Gibraltar on October 21, 1805. There the British war fleet, under Admiral Horatio Nelson defeated the Spanish and French in one of the great sea battles in world history. Admiral Nelson, aboard the flagship *Victory*, was killed during the battle. Nelson's body was returned to England in a cask of rum, the alcohol acting as a preservative. In

24

England he was buried in Westminster Abbey, and one of the world's most famous monuments was later erected to him in Trafalgar Square.

As Spain continued to decline in wealth and power, so did the condition of the majority of its people—the poor. There always were, in fact, just two main classes in Spain—the rich and the poor. The rich were members of the nobility, owners of the large estates, or leaders of the Roman Catholic church. The owners of the great estates kept the peasants poor through exorbitantly high land rentals. The church carefully guarded its income, which also came from large landholdings as well as from contributions and investments, to be used by the church fathers at their own discretion. There was almost no way that a poor Spaniard could hope to escape from poverty so long as the oppression of the monarchy and the church continued.

By the middle of the nineteenth century Spain had lost most of its overseas colonial empire except for Cuba, Puerto Rico, and the Philippines. These were later lost to the United States in the Spanish-American War of 1898. Closer to home Spain managed to hold on to Spanish Morocco and the Balearic Islands and Canary Islands.

But as the old Spain died, a new and more democratic Spain struggled to be born. Several futile attempts were made to eliminate the monarchy, establish a constitutional government, and turn the nation into a republic. These efforts caused constant revolutionary conflicts between liberals and conservatives.

The liberals were largely made up of anarchists, syndicalists, socialists, Communists, Republicans, and trade unionists. While these groups had various differences, their basic aim was to establish a constitutional government.

The conservatives were made up of army leaders, monarchists, great landowners, and a majority of the Roman Catholic church leaders. They opposed the establishment of a democratic republic and favored a continuation of the monarchy.

During World War I Spain remained neutral, and during this period the feuding between liberals and conservatives temporarily died down. A measure of prosperity was brought to the country by the sale of supplies to the Allied nations. But after the war Spain lost its foreign markets, and severe economic depression set in. This situation was further aggravated by the worldwide economic depression in the 1930s. Poverty among the rural population was severe, and in the cities jobs and wages fell to an all-time low. Unrest again became widespread.

During the postwar period an army officer, General Miguel Primo de Rivera, seized power by promising the king that he would restore order in the country by establishing a military directorate to run the government. Theoretically King Alfonso XIII was still head of government, but Primo de Rivera actually took over as

dictator. Primo's harsh reforms brought little improve-
ment in the Spanish economy, and soon the self-pro-
claimed dictator was forced to resign and flee to
France.

Once again a demand for constitutional republican
government arose, and there were revolutionary riots
throughout the country. Finally in 1931 national elections were held, and the liberal Republicans won an
overwhelming victory. The monarchy was thus brought
to an end. King Alfonso refused to abdicate, but he did
agree to leave the country. A provisional republican
government was formed with a president and a new
liberal constitution that separated church and state.
This government was, of course, strongly opposed by
the conservatives, the Nationalists.

One of the first things the new government did was
to seize many of the great estates that had been owned
by rich landowners and by the Roman Catholic church.
Under a new agrarian reform law these estates were
broken up and sold in cheap parcels to small farmers.
The new leaders also retaliated against the church,
which many felt had been too closely tied to the monarchy. Many churches, convents, and monasteries were
burned. All Roman Catholic schools were closed, and
many Jesuit priests and teachers were driven from the
country. With half of the Spanish people unable to
read or write, and tens of thousands of children out of
school, this latter move seemed especially ill-advised.
But the Spanish people who were now in power had

been so long oppressed that reason did not temper their actions.

The conservatives made every effort to reestablish the monarchy, but such efforts were quickly quelled and the monarchist leaders jailed or deported. But it was the conservatives who were the wealthy members of the Spanish populace, and the liberals had little or no money on which to run a government. This in itself created major problems.

A further problem had to do with the province of Catalonia's desire for independence. The Catalans, like the Basque people in the Pyrenees region of Spain and France, had long wanted to be independent. As soon as the new republic was declared, the Catalans wasted no time in proclaiming a separate "Catalonian State." While such a move threatened to cause turmoil in the rest of Spain, the new republican government decided it had little choice but to go along with the creation of a "republic within a republic," including the establishment of two co-official languages—Catalan in Catalonia and Castilian in the rest of Spain.

Gradually during the next two years disillusion with the experiment in republican government set in throughout Spain. Among other things, some type of education for about 350,000 schoolchildren had to be provided, and no real provisions were being made for this crisis.

Disillusion led to demands for yet another election, and in the fall of 1933 the liberals were voted out of office. In this election, for the first time, Spanish women were allowed to vote, and the seven million female votes strengthened the swing to the right.

Spanish women were among the most staunch supporters of the church, and they expected their children to receive a traditional Catholic education. They were thus inclined to vote against the Republicans and for a return to conservative, traditional Spanish government.

But the new Nationalist government managed to remain in power for only three years when a new election was demanded by the Republicans, who had recently regained power. Once again the Republicans were voted into office. But by now the differences between the two sides had become so great that civil war threatened the country.

# 4

▼▼

## ENTER THE ARMY
## AND
## GENERAL FRANCO

Immediately after the 1936 election armed conflict broke out between the conservative Nationalists and liberal Republicans. For six months, from February to July, men and women from both sides fought each other in the streets of Madrid, Barcelona, and many smaller cities and towns throughout the country. From the beginning the fighting was extremely cruel and ruthless, and this savagery was to mark the entire Civil War that followed. Men and women were dragged from their homes by armed bands and murdered in the streets. The Republican government made some futile attempts to stop the disturbances, but they continued more or less unabated.

The government was also faced with the problem of what to do about certain army leaders whom government officials knew to be disloyal. Instead of arresting these disloyal military men, the government simply transferred several of the leaders to remote posts outside the country. One of these transferred officers was General Francisco Franco, who was assigned to duty as military governor of the Canary Islands.

In 1936 the Spanish army numbered about 100,000 officers and men, 30,000 of whom were tough and well-trained troops in Spanish Morocco. A small group of Nationalist army officers was planning to overthrow the government. They were led by Generals Emilio Mola, José Sanjurjo, and Franco. Mola was the chief organizer of the conspiracy. Sanjurjo was selected as the man to be presented to the Spanish public as the nation's leader once the military coup succeeded. Franco was to be second in command of the Rebel forces under Mola. In the end it was Franco who not only led the rebellion but also became the nation's dictator.

Franco did not at first impress people as a military man. But in his case appearances were deceiving. He was a rather small man with a high-pitched, squeaky voice that did not carry well on the parade ground. At one of his first parades as an officer, however, one of the soldiers in the ranks made the mistake of making fun of Franco's voice, whereupon Franco took out his revolver and shot the would-be comic dead. After that when Commander Franco spoke, everybody listened. Franco was not even disciplined for his murderous action, because in the Spanish military insubordination, in whatever form, was considered punishable by death.

Francisco Franco Y Bahamonde (following Spanish

custom, his mother's family name, Bahamonde, was formally added to his surname) was born December 4, 1892, in El Ferrol, Galicia, Spain's northwesternmost province. His mother was Pilar Bahamonde. His father, Nicolás Franco, was a naval paymaster.

Franco's father wanted his son to go into the navy, but young Francisco decided to go into the army because ever since Spain's defeat in the Spanish-American War the country had few ships and fewer officer vacancies. Francisco entered the Spanish Military Academy in 1907 and was graduated in 1910. His fellow cadets never really understood the puritanical young Franco, who refused to drink, smoke, or even play cards with them. Clearly he had his eye on rapid promotion, because he made no effort to disguise his driving ambition.

Almost immediately after graduation young Franco was sent to Spanish Morocco, where he fought in the Spanish Foreign Legion against Riffian tribesmen who were trying to prevent the colonization of their homeland. Fighting between the Legion and the Riffs was savage. The Legionnaires' battle cry was "Long Live Death," and they fought with a kind of insane bravery. The Riffs too fought fiercely, asking no quarter and giving none. Both sides looted and mutilated their enemies' bodies. In one short battle the Spanish lost some 16,000 men. Franco himself was critically wounded when he was shot in the stomach during this battle. But his heroics gained him fame back in Spain, where he was greeted as "the ace of the Legion" when he returned there to recuperate from his wounds.

Franco had gone to Spanish Morocco when he was still in his late teens. At twenty-three he became a major and at thirty took command of the Legion. At thirty-four he was promoted to general, the youngest general in Europe at that time.

Despite his rapid rise in rank, however, Franco's fortunes seemed to rise and fall with the changing governments. King Alfonso XIII made him director of the military academy at Saragossa. But when Alfonso was forced to leave the country in 1931, the new Republican government sent Franco to the Balearic Islands. Back in power in 1933, the conservative Nationalists again restored Franco to military power as chief of staff to the minister of war.

It was while Franco was in the war ministry that he first openly displayed his hatred of Communists and all left-wing liberals. In 1934 there was a revolt against the government by the miners in the province of Asturias. Convinced that this revolt was led by Communist revolutionaries, Franco quickly moved army troops in to suppress it. Within two weeks the Asturian rebellion was put down, but in the process some 2,000 miners were killed and several thousand others wounded. For his brutality in effectively handling the Asturian revolt, Franco earned the nickname of "The Butcher" among Spanish workers.

In 1936, when the liberal Republicans returned to power, Franco was sent to his obscure post in the Canary Islands. It was from there that he began his true rise to power.

The Spanish Civil War actually began in Morocco when, on July 17 the military leaders there announced a revolution against the Spanish government. As a result, troops in garrisons throughout Spain revolted. At this point General Sanjurjo was killed in an airplane crash, and at Mola's request Franco took over as military leader of the revolt.

While General Mola and his aides had been making last-minute plans to seize the government, Franco had displayed a reluctance to leave the Canary Islands. So cautious had he been, in fact, that several of Mola's aides began referring to Franco as "Miss Canary Islands of 1936." But once the revolt was under way and General Sanjurjo was killed, Franco took command of the military action with a will. He immediately flew from the Canary Islands to Morocco. As soon as he was certain that Morocco was secure in Rebel hands, Franco flew to Spain on July 18 and established a Fascist government at Burgos.

By August 1, 1936, Franco and his Moroccan army forces, having been transferred to Burgos, were ready to begin their march on Madrid, the Spanish capital. Madrid, Franco predicted, would fall in just a few weeks. But by the time the Abraham Lincoln Brigade went into action, the Republican Loyalists in Madrid had successfully withstood the Rebel siege for more than six months. The Abraham Lincoln Brigade saw its first combat action in the Battle of Jarama in mid-February 1937.

# 5

▼▼

# THE BATTLE OF JARAMA

While they were in the midst of their first training, the Lincolns began to hear rumors that Franco's Rebels had broken through the Loyalist defenses in the Jarama River Valley just south of Madrid. The story soon spread that the American trainees were to be ordered to defend a key road between Valencia and Madrid. Vital supplies for the beleaguered capital city were sent from Valencia along this road.

At this time the Lincoln Brigade numbered about 450, although additional volunteers were arriving in Spain every day. These partially trained 450 men were to be used in support of a British battalion that had suffered severe casualties in the early fighting. Merriman, now a captain, had already divided the Lincolns into two rifle companies and a machine-gun company. Leaders had also been selected for each company, so there was some semblance of a chain of command among the rookie Americans.

The rumors about their going into action proved to be true. The Lincolns were assembled in the bullring at Albacete. Here they were given an emotional pep talk by the base commander, Marty, and issued helmets, new rifles, bayonets, and 150 rounds of ammunition apiece. These rifles—Remingtons made in the U.S. but shipped from Russia—like those issued earlier were covered with grease and had to be carefully cleaned before they could be used. Then Captain Merriman had to get special permission for his men to load and fire several shots from their new weapons so they would at least know a little about how to use them once they got into battle. This, of course, gave the men no chance to "zero in" their weapons—correctly align the front and rear sights and adjust the line of fire to make sure the rifles were firing accurately. Nevertheless, on the way to the front lines the men each fired several rounds into the surrounding countryside to make sure their weapons fired at all.

In the middle of the night some 45 trucks driven by Spanish civilians pulled up outside the Albacete bullring, and the men were ordered to board them. The convoy, with lights out, headed north toward the Jarama Valley and Madrid. As the trucks approached to within about ten miles of the key Madrid–Valencia road, the men began to hear the first sounds of battle— the distant boom of cannons and the rattle of machine-gun and small-arms fire. Before long they began to see the eternal waste of war—damaged trucks, stalled and burned-out cars, abandoned tanks—along the road and in nearby fields. Curiously, however, as the darkness waned and the sun rose, the men also saw many peasant farmers beginning to work their fields, ignoring the convoy and other signs of war around them.

As they drew a few miles closer to the battle zone in the Jarama Valley, the men of the Lincoln Brigade experienced their first direct attack. Several German Heinkel fighter-bomber aircraft suddenly appeared, flying just a few yards above the convoy, and began to strafe the trucks. Immediately the convoy was stopped and the men ran into the nearby fields and sprawled facedown on the ground.

When the Heinkels roared away, the Lincolns reassembled near their trucks and prepared once again to board them. But at this point an officer from Republican headquarters rode up in a command car and told Captain Merriman his men should take over a nearby hill. The men were also told to dig in as soon as possible, because they were now just a few hundred yards from the front lines and could expect to be shelled as soon as the Rebels located their position.

Immediately the men began to ask what they were supposed to dig in with.

"Use your bayonets and helmets," Captain Merriman told them.

There was much grumbling, but the men went to work digging holes for their own shelter. This work was speeded up by occasional and apparently random rifle fire that began to find its way onto the hillside. By the next day most of the men were out of sight below ground level. Here and there, however, a few men would raise their heads to see what was going on around them. When they did so they were warned by an observer, who lay half exposed in a shallow trench, to keep their heads down. This observer had been assigned by Captain Merriman to warn of any impending attack. His name was Charles Edwards.

"You gotta keep your heads down because there're snipers out there shooting at us," Edwards shouted.

"What about you?" somebody asked. "Don't you have to take cover?"

"I'm an exception," Edwards called back. "I'm an observer."

They were his last words. A moment later a bullet pierced his helmet and his skull, and Charles Edwards became the first member of the Abraham Lincoln Brigade to die in battle. The date was February 17, 1937.

At about the time Edwards was killed, the Rebels also unleashed an artillery barrage on the dug-in Lincolns. It was a terrifying experience, but none of the men broke and ran. In the midst of the barrage a second American died, struck by shrapnel from an artillery shell. He was Mark Chelebian, a New Yorker.

For the next several days the Lincolns underwent further punishment from enemy aircraft that strafed and bombed their position on what the men had now aptly nicknamed "Suicide Hill." But still they did not break and run. This fact in itself was impressive to both the Loyalists and Rebels. Up to now whenever front-line positions had been shelled, the occupants had fled. During their flight they always suffered severe casualties. But now it was seen that by digging in and holding their ground under intense fire, the Americans had suffered relatively few casualties—two dead and several men wounded.

On February 21 Merriman received orders to move his men to another nearby hill and prepare for an attack against the Rebel positions. The attack was scheduled for February 23. Its purpose was to drive the enemy from their entrenched position on a high ridge overlooking the main Valencia–Madrid road and thus make the road safe for Republican supply convoys to travel to Madrid.

Because of confusion among the commanders at Loyalist headquarters, the Lincolns did not receive orders to begin their attack until three o'clock in the afternoon. The day was dark and cold; nevertheless, the men started forward resolutely through a grove of olive trees. But fierce fire from the entrenched Rebels forced the Americans to stop and try to dig in almost immediately. To make matters worse a Spanish brigade on the Lincolns' left had failed to advance at all, thus exposing the entire American left flank to unrestricted fire.

Merriman had been told to remain at Loyalist headquarters during the attack. There he noted in his diary: "We could have broken through that night if we had been given support." As it was, the Lincolns remained hopelessly pinned down, and at ten o'clock orders came for them to retreat to their original positions. The withdrawal was especially frustrating to Merriman and his men, because the futile attack had cost them twenty men killed and forty wounded. Merriman vowed he would not let his men advance alone again.

The next day the leaden skies began to pour down rain on the surviving Lincolns huddled in their holes and shallow trenches. Not only were the men wet and miserably cold, but they were also hungry. Food had gotten to them only irregularly, and some men had not eaten in twenty-four hours. Captain Merriman concentrated his efforts on getting a hot meal, including coffee, to each of his men. Once this was accomplished, he returned to headquarters to learn what the new orders were.

Merriman was told that on February 27 his men were again to advance against the entrenched Fascists. But this time the Lincolns would definitely be supported by a replacement Spanish battalion on their left. In addition to artillery fire there would be Loyalist tanks and aircraft attacking the Rebels. Merriman noted in his diary that the plan seemed a sound one.

On the rainy morning of February 27 once again confusion at command headquarters delayed the start of the attack. This time Merriman was with his men at his own hillside headquarters, and he saw the Spanish battalion on his left leave its trenches about ten A.M.

despite an almost complete lack of supporting artillery fire. But the Spanish advanced only a short way before many of them went down from enemy fire. The rest quickly retreated to their original positions.

Merriman immediately got on the phone to command headquarters and spoke with a Colonel Vladimir Copič, who was supposed to be coordinating the attack. Copič was a volunteer from Yugoslavia. Merriman told him the Spanish advance had already failed, and what was more, there were no tanks or Loyalist aircraft in evidence. And what had happened to the artillery?

Copič said there would be a delay but artillery fire and tanks would soon be coming. The weather made flying almost impossible, so there might not be any air support, but Merriman and his Lincoln Brigade must be prepared to advance no matter what kind of support he and his men had.

Merriman, of course, objected. He insisted that without the advance of the Spanish on his left, the Lincoln attack could not go forward.

Copič ordered Merriman to attack "at all costs." The ridge must be taken by the Americans. Copič also said he was sending two of his aides to the Lincoln Brigade site to make sure his orders were carried out.

Merriman realized he could be court-martialed and shot if he continued to disagree. He had done all he could to save his men. Now all he could do was prepare them for the attack—and personally lead them.

By now it was almost noon. Merriman gave a few

last-minute orders, then strode along the trench and vaulted up on top of the protective earth embankment. Pumping his arm up and down in the traditional infantry advance signal, he shouted at his men to follow him. To a man they left their shelter holes and entrenchments and advanced toward the enemy.

Merriman was perhaps halfway to the enemy positions when a machine-gun bullet shattered his shoulder. He stumbled forward a few paces and then went down. Immediately two of Merriman's men grabbed him by the ankles and hauled him behind an olive tree and out of the line of fire.

Although severely wounded, Merriman was still conscious. Soon a first-aid man dressed his wound and managed to get him back to the shallow American trench from which he had started. He refused to be evacuated, however, until he had officially passed on the command of the battalion. Merriman's second in command, Douglas Seacord, had already been killed. Next in line was Lt. Philip Cooperman. Merriman officially ordered Cooperman to take over command of the Lincoln Brigade and to make certain its command post was protected. Then Merriman allowed himself to be carried by stretcher to the nearest battlefield aid station.

Despite the fact that it was taking heavy casualties, the remainder of the Lincoln Brigade continued its slow but relentless advance until three o'clock in the afternoon. Then a deluge of rain struck, and in the face of this storm and the storm of steel from the enemy trenches, the Lincolns broke off their attack. Slowly, the few able-bodied men who were left, along with the walking wounded, drifted back to their starting positions and the relative safety of the shelter holes and trenches. Fewer than a hundred Americans had not become casualties. Another hundred were killed— among them a young Iowa-Dakota lad named Max Marek—and the rest were wounded.

But, badly mauled as it was, the Lincoln Brigade was not withdrawn from frontline duty. Gradually, newly trained recruits were fed back into its ranks to build the battalion up to strength. Fortunately, while this rebuilding process was going on, Franco's Rebels did not launch any major attacks against the Americans. For many weeks, however, skirmishing did continue between the two sides in the Jarama Valley, and fighting did not end there until late June, with neither side a clear winner. Then the newly reconstituted Lincoln Brigade was thrown into fierce fighting even closer to Madrid, at Brunete.

Out of their tragic losses in the Battle of Jarama the Lincolns sang to the tune of "Red River Valley" a song that went:

> *There's a valley in Spain called Jarama;*
> *It's a place that we all know too well,*
> *For 'tis there that we wasted our manhood*
> *And most of our old age as well.*

45

Captain Merriman first heard this song while he was recovering from the successful operation on his shattered shoulder at the base hospital, the Hospitale d'Internationale, in the town of Murcia. Its melancholy air made him more determined than ever to recover from his wound as quickly as possible so he could return to the Lincolns and lead the battalion as a truly successful fighting unit.

Helping Captain Merriman recover from his wound was his wife, Marion. In Moscow on March 2, 1937, she had received a telegram from her husband that read simply: "Wounded. Come at once." She had immediately left Russia for Spain.

# 6

▼▼

## MARION MERRIMAN JOINS THE LINCOLN BRIGADE

European airline travel was still in a relatively primitive and uncertain state in the late 1930s. Consequently, Marion Merriman flew only from Moscow to Königsberg, Germany. Rough weather and delays made her miss the connection to Paris, and she was forced to travel to Paris by train. There it took her several days to get a visa permitting her entry into Spain. (The delay was due to the fact that a Spanish Civil War international nonintervention pact technically barred all foreigners from entering Spain. This pact had recently been signed by the United States, France, and Great Britain, but it was never strictly adhered to by any of the signing nations.) Once in Spain she wasn't exactly sure where to go to find her husband until a newspaper reporter told her he was in the hospital at Murcia, not far from Valencia.

Marion expected to find her husband a bedridden patient. She was pleasantly surprised and greatly relieved to find him walking about in the hospital talking with the other patients, most of whom were wounded members of the Lincoln Brigade. His shattered shoulder, however, was encased in a cast that extended to his waist, against which his arm was immobilized. Since there had been no medical plaster available from which to fashion this cast, the doctors had been forced to use ordinary building construction plaster, so the cast was extraordinarily heavy. But Merriman did not seem to mind the extra discomfort—and the cast did not hinder the warm greeting he gave his wife.

In their first days together after their reunion Marion tentatively broached the possibility of his returning to the United States once he was well enough to travel.

Merriman stubbornly refused. He told his wife he was needed in Spain.

Marion knew there would be no changing his mind. But she told her husband that if he was staying, she was too.

Merriman did not argue with her. But he pointed out that it would be difficult for her to remain.

It turned out, however, not to be so difficult as they both imagined. First of all Marion went to work as a volunteer in the hospital. She wrote letters to the friends and relatives of the hospitalized Lincoln Brigade men, many of whom had not written to or heard from anyone in the United States in weeks. She also worked as a nurse's aide. And, she acted as a spokesperson for her husband with the many reporters who wanted information about him. Merriman's being wounded in battle had made headlines in American West Coast newspapers. He personally disliked playing the role of war hero but realized publicity about the war might swell the numbers of American volunteers. Such publicity also resulted in cash contributions to the Loyalist cause.

Meanwhile, Captain Merriman was checking with officials of the International Brigades to see if his wife could remain in Spain as a war volunteer. Finally he was told that she could. But to do so Marion would have to join the XV International Brigade and swear she would never volunteer for frontline combat duty. Loyalist officials feared the adverse publicity that would result if an American woman were killed in Spain. Marion readily agreed and was sworn in as a corporal in the rebuilding Abraham Lincoln Brigade—its only female member. She had to have a uniform especially made for her by a seamstress in Valencia, and she was issued an official Sam Browne belt and the stock hemp-soled sandals or *espadrilles*.

Several weeks after Marion's induction into the Lincoln Brigade, the Merrimans were ordered to return to Albacete. Marion remained there in the International Brigade headquarters doing clerical work, but Captain Merriman was transferred to another training base at nearby Tarazona, where the newest Lincoln Brigade recruits were now being trained. There were soon enough new American volunteers to form a second unit, this one called the Washington Battalion. Canadian volunteers were also now arriving in great numbers, so a Canadian unit named after two Canadian patriots, Alexander Mackenzie and Louis Papineau, was formed. Merriman, despite his awkward plaster arm cast, also took overall charge of the Washington Battalion and the Canadian Battalion, the latter having been promptly nicknamed the "Mac-Paps."

Due to his expanding command, Merriman was soon promoted to major and named temporary chief of staff of the XV International Brigade. He at first resisted the promotion, because he feared it would confine him to administrative duties at Brigade headquarters. He was assured, however, that he would again lead his men into combat once his shoulder wound had fully healed and the cast was removed.

Meanwhile, Major Merriman and his wife were placed on temporary duty in Madrid, where a propaganda radio broadcast to the United States was being planned. The Merrimans' participation in this broadcast had been requested by author Ernest Hemingway, who was one of the volunteers in charge of raising funds for the Loyalist cause. Hemingway was also taking part in the production of a propaganda film, *The Spanish Earth*, in which an actual combat scene at a besieged bridge would give the author the idea for the key final episode in his novel *For Whom the Bell Tolls.* And the inspiration for the novel's hero, Robert Jordan, apparently came to Hemingway at the first meeting between him and Merriman in Madrid. Hemingway, of course, had heard of Merriman's exploits for several months, but it was in Madrid that the two men first met.

# 7
▼▼

# THE SIEGE OF MADRID

The Spanish Civil War has often been called the opening battle or testing ground of World War II. Nowhere was this more apparent than in the attempt, for the first time in the history of warfare, to force cities to surrender through the use of unrestricted aerial bombardment.

The first major city on which this experiment was tried was Madrid. The experiment failed there as it was to fail in other large urban centers in the future— Barcelona later in the Spanish Civil War; London, Berlin, and Stalingrad in World War II; Hanoi in the Vietnam War. Although Tokyo and several other Japanese cities were hit with conventional bombs, it was only when *atomic* bombs were dropped on Hiroshima and Nagasaki in World War II that aerial warfare succeeded in bringing about Japan's surrender. The use of conventional bombs in aerial warfare has usually increased enemy resistance. Certainly Madrid's resistance in the Spanish Civil War was greatly strengthened by Franco's use of unrestricted aerial bombardment.

There were, however, certain exceptions to this general rule as far as Spain was concerned. Smaller population centers—villages and towns—could be virtually blown off the face of the earth and their inhabitants killed or driven from the area. One such Spanish town was Guernica in the Pyrenees region. This area was the home of the freedom-loving and highly independent Basque people. Although Guernica had a population of only some 7,000, Basques from all over the region regarded it as the home of Basque liberties. At the center of the town was a famous oak tree beneath which Basque individual rights had frequently been sworn to by Spanish kings.

Soon after General Franco and his Fascists revolted against the government, Franco decided that one of the quickest ways to impress the Spanish people with the strength of the Rebels would be to dramatically defeat the Basques in battle. The battle, however, would not be a traditional infantry attack but an aerial bombardment. The fact that the Basques had no anti-aircraft guns and that this would make such an attack wholly one-sided and scarcely a battle at all did not deter General Franco. Obliterating Guernica, the heart of Spanish independence, would serve as an object lesson to the rest of Loyalist Spain.

For his brutal aerial attack, which was also something of an experiment in warfare since it had never been tried before, Franco and his aides had at their command 20 Heinkel He.111 and 15 Junkers Ju.52 bombers. Also available was a squadron of five fighter planes. All these aircraft and their pilots had been sent to Spain by German dictator Adolf Hitler and his *Luft-waffe* (air force) commander, Hermann Göring. Hitler and Göring were not only interested in aiding would-be dictator Franco and his Fascists; they also wanted to find out just how well German combat aircraft would perform in actual aerial warfare. These German pilots and their planes were a part of the *Luftwaffe*'s famed Condor Legion.

On April 26, 1937, at around five o'clock in the evening, German bombers began their aerial bombardment of Guernica. They were followed up by fighter aircraft, which machine-gunned the streets. Both 1,000-pound incendiary and 500-pound explosive bombs were dropped by waves of aircraft that arrived at twenty-minute intervals. This system of pattern bombing in waves was worked out by Göring as the most effective method of destroying a major target. Bombing in waves enabled each successive wave to attack targets missed by preceding waves.

When darkness fell and the raid ended, the flames disclosed that the entire center of Guernica had been destroyed. Later it was learned that more than 1,600 people had been killed and some 900 wounded. The rest of the town's population fled into the surrounding countryside. Interestingly, the town's famous Independence Oak Tree was undamaged.

The next day outcries arose from all over Spain—from all over the world, in fact. In Paris artist Pablo Picasso, who had been born in Málaga, Spain, but now lived in France, immediately began work on a huge mural, twenty-five feet by eleven feet, depicting the horrors of modern warfare as symbolized by the destruction of Guernica. He completed it in a month. Picasso's *Guernica* is now widely regarded as one of the artist's masterpieces.

It was not surprising that when Franco's forces failed to capture the Spanish capital in a few weeks, as he had at first predicted, the Rebel commander resorted to increased aerial bombardment as the means to force a decision. It had worked wonderfully well at Guernica, so why shouldn't it work on a larger scale in Madrid?

The planes and pilots he called on to do the job were once again those of the German Condor Legion. The planes were 20 Junkers bombers and, this time, some 30 fighter planes. Machine-gunning the terrified population of Guernica had proved marvelously effective in driving the people from town. In Madrid Franco envisioned mass panic in the streets in the face of machine-gun attacks from *Luftwaffe* fighter aircraft.

The German bombers rained down incendiary- and explosive-bomb destruction on Madrid for an initial twenty-four-hour period—again in waves, but this time at half-hour intervals. Changing the time between waves was done to confuse would-be rescuers trying to aid the wounded. The people of Madrid had never before been the victims of any kind of bombardment. Isolated from World War I, they had rarely seen airplanes at all, and certainly no bombers. Consequently, they reacted to the bombardment and subsequent machine-gunning with some degree of panic at first. But it wasn't long before they were rallied by a few of their leaders, both military and civilian, to respond to this attack with outrage and with a fierce determination to defend their city, in hand-to-hand fighting if necessary, from any infantry invasion that might follow the aerial bombardment itself. It soon became apparent, though, that aerial bombardment could not possibly destroy a city of millions of people and hundreds of thousands of buildings as Guernica had been destroyed. Soon people began going underground to protect themselves from future air raids, and this became the pattern of all defense against urban bombardment—that and striking back with antiaircraft guns and night fighter aircraft. Night fighter aircraft, however, were not in use until World War II.

The Spanish capital had some antiaircraft batteries but not many. Their number, however, was increased throughout the war. On the ground Madrid was defended by some of the military who had remained loyal to the government; by the civil guard, which was a kind of police militia; and by civilians. In the end it was the civilians or citizen-soldiers who saved the day for as long as it could be saved.

One of the civilian leaders was the heroic woman Dolores Ibarruri, who was generally known as "La Pasionaria." When Ernest Hemingway first arrived in Madrid and took up residence at the Florida Hotel, he almost immediately became familiar with the tales of La Pasionaria's heroic resistance efforts. Eventually he would use her as the inspiration for one of the leading figures in *For Whom the Bell Tolls*: She became the model for the guerrilla fighter called Pilar, who befriends the American Robert Jordan and aids him on his lone bridge-blowing efforts on behalf of the Loyalists.

Dolores Ibarruri was one of eleven children of a Basque coal-mining family. She believed her family as well as other mining families were being exploited by the rich mineowners. Forced to quit school at fourteen because of poverty, she began traveling from village to village speaking out against this exploitation. To earn a living she sold sardines from a large basket she carried on her head, and worked as a dressmaker's assistant and as a waitress. Married in her early teens—her husband was also a miner—Ibarruri had six children, four of whom died in infancy from what she regarded as lack of proper medical care.

Ibarruri had been raised as a Catholic, but in her twenties she left the church and became a professional agitator, first for the Socialists and then for the Communists. Her rabble-rousing speeches landed her in jail several times, but she continued her political trouble-making. Twice, Russian leaders invited her to Moscow, where she received training in revolutionary methods.

Dolores Ibarruri, or La Pasionaria, was a revolutionary against the monarchy, and she was bitterly opposed to Franco and his Fascists. What she wanted was a form of popular government in which all people had a voice. Consequently, although she was indeed a professed Communist and stoutly opposed to the capitalist form of government as well as the Catholic church, she was a staunch member of the Popular Front, which supported the Loyalist Republican government. The Popular Front was the name given the disparate group of Loyalist organizations opposed to Fascism.

Early in her political career Ibarruri adopted the name La Pasionaria, or "passion flower," as a pen name for a series of newspaper articles. These political tracts, she later explained, were written during Easter week— the week of "La Pasion."

La Pasionaria was a striking-looking woman when Hemingway and the Merrimans first came to know her and learned of her exploits in Madrid. At that time she was in her early forties. A severely erect woman, she was also tall for a Basque—most Basques are short in stature. Her raven-black hair was combed back and pinned in a bun. Her dress was always black, and had been since her grandmother had died when Ibarruri was twenty. "I began dressing in mourning then and never stopped," she told her new friends. "Besides, how could I, a miner's wife, go out dressed in burgundy red?"

Observers, however, frequently pointed out that the black dress was probably also worn for dramatic effect, for by now La Pasionaria had become a somber symbol of sacrifice and resistance known not only in besieged Madrid but also throughout the rest of Loyalist Spain.

La Pasionaria began her rise to fame on the evening that Franco announced his first attack on Madrid and prematurely predicted the capital's fall. That night the government parliament met in extraordinary session, which was broadcast via radio to the entire nation. La Pasionaria was one of a mere handful of Communist members elected to this parliament, but already she had begun to become an important voice in it.

On this particular night she took over one of the microphones and, as historian Hugh Thomas has pointed out, "broadcast the first of many violent speeches in the Civil War demanding resistance throughout the country, urging the women of Spain to fight with knives and burning oil, and ending with the slogan, 'It is better to die on your feet than to live on your knees! *¡No pasaran!*' (They shall not pass)." The last cry, which was first credited to a French general— *"Ils ne passeront pas"*—in rallying his troops against the Germans at Verdun in World War I, immediately became the chief rallying cry of the Spanish Republic in its fight against the Fascists.

When the Merrimans arrived in Madrid, in April, 1937, the city had become a makeshift fortress. Barricades had been thrown up in all the streets to prevent the free movement of Fascist tanks if the enemy should succeed in breaking into the city, an event that was not to occur until two and a half years after the start of the Spanish Civil War.

Food and ammunition were always in short supply during the siege of Madrid. That supplies were available at all was due to the heroic fighting of loyal Spanish soldiers aided by the International Brigades in general and the Abraham Lincoln Brigade in particular in keeping open the Valencia–Madrid road and the other main roads that led into the capital.

Within the city the biggest fear in the beginning was that the Loyalists might be betrayed by traitorous Fascist sympathizers in their midst. Not all of Madrid's citizens were Loyalists by any means, but the number of traitors eventually proved to be much smaller than originally suspected. This was a miscalculation made not only by the Loyalists but also by the Rebel Nationalists. At one time when the Fascists first began their attack on Madrid, Fascist General Emilio Mola was in charge of an army command that was advancing in four separate columns. "I also have a fifth column inside Madrid," he said in a radio address, meaning, of course, Fascist sympathizers within the capital. Since then "fifth column" has come to mean any secret supporters of the enemy, and a fifth columnist is one who engages in espionage and subversive activities within his or her own country out of sympathy with an enemy.

Merriman and Hemingway spent several of their first hours together comparing notes on the war. Merriman filled Hemingway in on the status of the XV International Brigade, and Hemingway in turn gave the major an overall picture of the war as he had seen it up to now. It was Hemingway's opinion, Merriman later told Marion, that the Republican Loyalists stood a good chance of winning the war—but only if they got considerably more help from outside sources. And that was the purpose of the radio propaganda broadcast to the United States.

Besides Hemingway there were other writers who would take part in the broadcast—John Dos Passos, who rivaled Hemingway as a post-World War I novelist; Josephine Herbst, a magazine writer who had recently become popular as a novelist; and Martha Gellhorn, a correspondent for *Collier's* magazine, to whom *For Whom the Bell Tolls* would be dedicated and who would later become Hemingway's wife.

Major Merriman was to be the high point of the broadcast. Hemingway would act as announcer, giving a background picture of the war; Dos Passos, Herbst, and Gellhorn would follow, giving the writers' view of the conflict, and Merriman would conclude with the actual combatant's picture. The Lincoln Brigade had already captured the romantic imagination of many Americans, and its battle-wounded commander was certain to attract an audience.

Major Merriman spent considerable time preparing his six-minute segment of the broadcast, pointing out that the war was more than a civil war. It was a conflict over the basic and simple question of whether people should be free, in Spain, and throughout the world. To this he added an appeal, not only for more volunteers— a request that was technically illegal—but also for cash to support the Loyalist cause.

On the night of the broadcast, the participants drove to a secret radio station in Madrid. Its location was kept hidden, and it had frequently been moved to avoid destruction by aerial bombardment. The broadcast went exceedingly well, Major Merriman thought, and he was especially pleased that at the last minute two other members of the Lincoln Brigade had also been obtained as participants. They were Dr. William Pike, the battalion physician, and Martin Hourihan, who was the most recent in a succession of several commanders of the battalion since Merriman had been made a staff officer.

There was no way of telling, of course, how successful the broadcast had been, but several times in ensuing months new Lincoln Brigade volunteers made a point of telling Major Merriman that he had been the inspiration for their coming to Spain.

The day after the broadcast Major Merriman and Marion returned to the volunteer training area. Soon Merriman had the cast removed from his arm and began to prepare once again to lead his men into battle.

Marion Merriman (front center), Robert Hale Merriman (left), and four other members of the Lincoln Brigade at the hospital in Murcia, Spain. Merriman's left arm and shoulder are in a cast, as he was recuperating from a bullet wound sustained during the Battle of Jarama.

This ambulance was purchased with funds contributed by Chicagoans who were sympathetic to the Loyalist cause in the Spanish Civil War. The U.S. State Department reported that during the war over two million dollars in aid was contributed to the Loyalists by some twenty-six American relief organizations.

General Francisco Franco (center) being saluted by members of the diplomatic corps in Burgos.

Loyalist forces charge up a hill to wipe out a Rebel machine gun nest.

A Loyalist soldier killed in action.

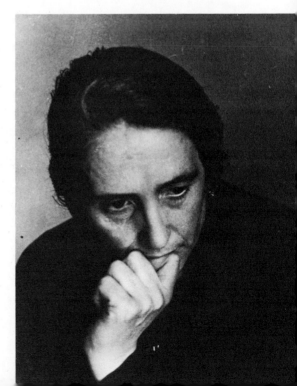

Dolores Ibarruri—
"La Pasionaria."

A street in Madrid after Rebel bombing. (Twisted rails and wreckage here show that much of the streetcar service in the city was destroyed.)

Thousands of Madrid's inhabitants—men, women, and children—sought refuge in subway stations from Rebel air attacks.

# 8
▼▼

## BACK INTO BATTLE

The Lincoln Brigade went back into battle, this time at Brunete just 19 miles west of Madrid, in July of 1937. It was accompanied by the recently formed Washington Battalion. The action at Brunete was much closer to Madrid than had been the action in the Jarama Valley, and it was thus much more important than ever that the Rebels be stopped. Otherwise they might break through into the streets of Madrid.

Over his strong objections the convalescent Major Merriman was not allowed to take part in the Brunete action. Martin Hourihan, who had briefly commanded the Lincoln Brigade, had been promoted to be a regimental aide to Major Merriman. Steve Nelson, a thirty-four-year-old shipyard worker from Philadelphia, was actually the new commissar of the Lincolns but was in overall charge of the battalion during the battle. Commissar Stember had been transferred to another unit in training. Oliver Law, a popular black captain from Chicago, was in charge of the Washington Battalion. Although he had served for six years in the U.S. Army before coming to Spain, this was the first time he had been given any authority, becoming the first American black to command whites in any military organization.

To begin with, the Brunete battle was intended to be a single part of a major Loyalist offensive campaign. And to begin with, the campaign was wholly successful.

Brunete was at a key position on the front west of Madrid. If it could be captured, the Rebels besieging the capital from the west could probably be cut off from a main body of Rebel troops that had been scoring major military successes to the north of the capital.

The method for dividing the Rebel front was for Loyalist troops to advance west along the Madrid–El Escorial road—another supply route to the capital—and then turn south and capture the sleepy little town of Brunete, population 1,500. Once Brunete was captured, it could be used as an anchor for future Loyalist attacks to keep the several miles of Rebel front divided. Spearheading the attack against Brunete itself were to be the Lincoln and Washington Battalions and a British battalion.

The Loyalists had been planning this offensive for more than two months and had at their command some tens of thousands of troops—virtually the entire strength of the Republican armed forces at this time. They were supported by more than 100 tanks and 100 aircraft, all of them from either France or Russia. By now France, although still neutral, was secretly sending military matériel to the Loyalists.

On July 6 the Loyalists began their advance across the desert-dry Castilian plain. The westward advance up the Madrid–El Escorial Road took two days. Those who made the march and the subsequent advance toward Brunete were later to recall how desperate they had all been for water as they struggled forward through the fierce hundred-degree heat of Spanish summer. "Even the rivers ran dry," one of the Americans, Edwin Rolfe, later wrote. He was referring to the Guadarrama River, normally a relatively large, fast-moving stream but now nothing but a dried-up riverbed. Nelson and Law had their men dig into the bed of the dry Guadarrama, but they found only a few canteenfuls of brackish water that the men said tasted of dead mules. Nevertheless they drank a few mouthfuls each.

Rebels on the Madrid–El Escorial road north of Brunete were taken by surprise by the opening phases of the Loyalist attack, but they did not panic. On the ground their forces were outnumbered perhaps three to one, but reinforcements were hurried to the battle. In addition to infantry reinforcements there were substantial numbers of planes from the Condor Legion as well as Savoia bombers from Italy and tanks from both Germany and Italy.

On the third day, when the three international battalions turned south toward Brunete, they ran into

71

massive resistance from the dug-in Rebels. Nevertheless, Nelson and Law led their men forward and by
evening charged into the northern edges of Villanueva
de la Cañada, a village just a few miles north of Brunete. The next day Brunete itself fell.

In these four days of fighting the Lincoln and Washington Battalions suffered some 50-percent casualties.
It was quickly decided to combine the two decimated
battalions into one full-strength Lincoln Brigade with
Captain Law in command. Unfortunately, Law was
shot in the stomach a short time later and died within
hours. This left Nelson in charge. Captain Law was not
the first American black to die in the Spanish Civil
War. That distinction went to an artist, Alonzo Wat-
son, who was killed in the Battle of Jarama.

Elsewhere on the front the Loyalist attack went
slowly forward for two weeks and then stalled. In Brunete the Lincolns consolidated their position and
began to prepare for a Rebel counterattack, which they
knew would soon come.

The Rebel counterattack built up gradually. Late in
July the Rebels attacked simultaneously all along the
front, using tanks to spearhead their advances. It was
in the use of tanks that the Loyalists were outmaneu-
vered here and elsewhere throughout the war. The
Loyalists always used their tanks in World War I fashion, spread out in support of, or advancing with, the
infantry. The Rebel tanks—at the insistence of the
German commander, General Kurt von Thoma—were

tightly bunched together to make a concentrated smash at one point in the Loyalist line until a break-through could be achieved.

Once this so-called *Schwerpunkt* (thrust point) was penetrated, the breakthrough was then exploited, with the German-commanded Rebel tanks fanning out in several directions to overwhelm the off-balance enemy. This tactic was the basic tactic of *Blitzkrieg* (lightning war) used by the Germans in overwhelming the Poles, French, and British early in World War II. In World War II the Germans added close air support to the blitzing tanks to thoroughly disrupt the enemy de-fenses.

By the end of July the Rebels had recaptured most of the territory they had originally lost to the Loyalists, including Brunete. The Loyalists had gained a total of fewer than 20 square miles at the cost of some 25,000 casualties, 80 percent of their tanks, and more than a third of their aircraft. The Lincoln Brigade, after it was combined with the Washington Battalion, suffered a casualty rate of 10 percent. The Rebels suffered about 17,000 casualties, and their other losses in matériel were also proportionately lower.

Nevertheless, both sides declared victory in the Bru-nete carnage just as they had after the Battle of Jarama.

Major Merriman had followed the battle closely from brigade headquarters. He had nothing but praise for the heroism displayed by the Americans, but he was heartsick at their heavy losses. When Steve Nelson returned to Albacete with the Lincoln survivors, they were warmly greeted by both Major Merriman and his wife, Marion, who made a point of visiting all the American wounded in the hospitals throughout the area.

Steve Nelson and his weary men settled quickly and luxuriously into their several weeks of rest and recuperation from battle, but soon Major Merriman was calling upon Nelson to confer with him about plans for proposed action farther to the north and east of Madrid. This was to be the Aragon offensive, in which the Lincolns and Major Merriman were scheduled to play vital roles.

# 9
▾▾

# THE ARAGON OFFENSIVE

In late August 1937 the Loyalists launched a diversionary offensive north and east of Madrid. The purpose of this offensive was to draw or divert Franco's troops away from Madrid.

The entire XV International Brigade was to take part in this offensive. Major Merriman, although he had recently been officially named the XV Brigade's chief of staff, was to actively lead the Internationals in combat. He was to be closely assisted by Brigade Commissar Steve Nelson.

The Lincoln Brigade was now led by a huge and tough Swede from Wisconsin, Hans Amlie. The British battalion was led by an Irish Communist, Peter Daley. The Canadian Mackenzie-Papineau or "Mac-Pap" Battalion now had a number of Americans in it and was, in fact, headed by two Yanks, Captain Bill Thompson and Commissar Joe Dallet. There was also a combined battalion made up of the Spanish 24th and the Yugoslav Dimitros Battalion. The commander of the XV Brigade, the Yugoslav Vladimir Copič, was also nominally in charge of the Spanish-Yugoslav unit.

Ever since the Battle of Jarama, where Major Merriman thought Copič mismanaged the attack orders, Merriman had little or no respect for Commander Copič. The two kept out of each other's way as much as possible. Merriman's opinion was shared by many of the men in the XV Brigade, but they had little choice but to continue to fight under Copič's overall command in the Aragon offensive. They were relieved, however, that Merriman was to be their immediate combat commander.

The Lincolns and the rest of the XV International Brigade began their movement from Albacete toward the general assembly area in Valencia on August 19. Even though they had known for weeks that the Aragon offensive was about to begin, the Internationals were not quite ready when the jump-off time came. Many of the men were in Madrid, either on leave or still in various hospitals recovering from wounds. To remedy this situation Major Merriman immediately sent an urgent message to one of the most reliable of the Lincoln Brigade veterans, Edwin Rolfe. The message read:

> *Paul* [the messenger delivering the note to Rolfe] *is responsible for bringing all the men possible from our brigade who remain in Ma-*

*drid on leave. All nationalities. You must help
him. Get him dry rations for the men to eat
on the way. Also a* Salvo Conducto [safe con-
duct] *for all ten trucks. The food is important.
Help him—he must get close to 200 men and
do it fast.*

*Merriman.*

Rolfe and Paul immediately went into action, going
from hotel to hotel and waking up all the Lincolns.
They then scurried about, rounding up gasoline, two
hundred loaves of bread, and cans of meat and sardines.

Within less than twelve hours Rolfe and Paul had
cobbled together a convoy of trucks—nothing short of
a miracle in beleaguered Madrid—and 192 volunteers.
Soon they joined with the rest of the Internationals
who had left their training bases, also by truck, and
were heading for Valencia.

At Valencia the men camped in the bullring for two
days. Here they were told the specific targets for their
forthcoming attack. The brigade would be heading
north toward Quinto and Belchite, two heavily forti-
fied towns in the Aragon region. The ultimate goal,
however, was the major city of Saragossa.

From Valencia the men moved out on trains. The
troop cars had machine guns on their roofs as defense
against strafing aircraft. The men drew lots to decide
who would man these machine guns while the train was
moving—a hair-raising job, especially since there were

several tunnels en route. Their first destination was the town of Hijar. Here they received a welcome supply of new Russian light machine guns. These weapons were much easier to carry and to fire once they were in place than any automatic weapons they had so far been issued.

During the last week in August the Lincoln Brigade occupied a high area near Purburell Hill within sight of the town of Quinto, their first enemy target. Purburell Hill itself was occupied by the enemy. From this strategic point they commanded all of the approaches to the town.

Between Purburell Hill and Quinto there was a flat, level plain about 200 yards wide. Beyond this plain and on either side of Quinto were Rebel fortifications. On the morning of August 25 the Lincolns started across this plain as part of a general attack. Against light opposition the Lincolns quickly crossed the plain until they came to an olive grove. Here they were suddenly pinned down by enfilading fire (crossfire) from the enemy fortifications flanking the city and by machine-gun fire from atop Purburell Hill. From the olive grove they watched the Yugoslav and British battalions attack Purburell Hill. The Mac-Pap Battalion remained in reserve.

But the Rebels were so thoroughly entrenched on the Purburell heights that they were impossible to dislodge. Nevertheless, most of their machine guns, which had been trained directly down on the Lincolns, were silenced by nightfall of the first day. That night the Lincolns lay awake awaiting a Rebel counterattack. None came.

The following morning at dawn the Lincoln Brigade, braving the enfilading fire from the flanking fortifications, managed to gain a toehold at the edge of Quinto. Once they were inside the town, opposition diminished somewhat, but the Americans still had to engage in fierce house-to-house fighting to dislodge the enemy. Using grenades and gasoline-filled bottles as weapons, they gradually began to clear out a major section of the town. As soon as they were able, they headed for high ground within the city, where Loyalist artillery could be placed and used to fire down upon the Rebels still holding out on Purburell Hill outside the town.

Once this high ground was attained, Major Merriman and his staff established brigade headquarters in Quinto. Within twenty-four hours the Rebels on Purburell Hill surrendered. They were without water, and the heavy pounding from the Loyalist artillery made the Rebel position untenable. Even so Major Merriman and his men were astonished at the number of Rebels—some 500—who surrendered and how well equipped they were.

The rest of Quinto was taken over by the whole XV Brigade during the next several days. During the fighting for the town there were only a handful of International casualties, while several hundred Rebels were killed and 1,000 captured. But there could be little time for celebration. Ahead lay the town of Belchite, which must be captured if the campaign against Saragossa were to be successful—and Belchite had not even fallen to the virtually unbeatable Napoleon in the Peninsular Wars in 1812. It had remained a stronghold ever since.

Belchite was strategically important because the crossroads at its center led into Saragossa and the rest of Aragon. In addition, one of these crossroads led directly into Madrid. Belchite was also one of the richest towns in Spain, a resort area for wealthy Spaniards, and its capture would be a morale coup for the Loyalists.

The battle for Belchite lasted six days, beginning near the end of August and ending during the first week in September.

On the first day the Lincolns were the point, or lead, battalion in the attack.

German engineers serving with the Rebels had supervised the construction of fortifications defending the city. These fortifications consisted of concrete-and-steel pillbox gun emplacements and iron stakes driven into the ground to serve as antitank and anti-infantry barriers.

Despite these formidable defenses, by nightfall of the first day the Lincolns had gained entry into the town. As soon as this was achieved, Major Merriman moved his command post inside the city limits and established headquarters under a concrete viaduct.

This viaduct was a bridge over part of the aqueduct system that had originally been built by the Romans when they had occupied this area of Spain centuries earlier. The aqueducts here and elsewhere were still in operation, furnishing water to much of the populace.

On the second day of fighting major Rebel opposition seemed to center at a church near the Belchite–Madrid road. Here a battalion of Rebels had barricaded themselves in and blocked the Loyalist advance. The church was built of rock and boulders and was a seemingly impregnable fortress.

At first Merriman ordered his men to circle around the church and continue their attack beyond it. But this was difficult, because there was only open ground on either side of the church, and as soon as troops tried to advance across this open ground, they were mowed down by machine-gun fire.

Merriman then ordered a frontal assault on the church, but American casualties mounted as each new wave of attackers was beaten back. Among the casualties, unfortunately, was Merriman's aide, Steve Nelson, who was shot in the face and groin and rescued only after a dozen men risked their lives to bring him from the field of fire to protective cover.

The second day ended in a stalemate. Early on the morning of the third day the recently named commander of the Lincoln Brigade, Hans Amlie, was also wounded. He was replaced by his aide, Leonard Lamb, a labor organizer from Brooklyn.

By the end of the third day the situation at the church had reached a critical impasse that was holding up the entire advance. That night Major Merriman and his aides puzzled over what their next effort should be. Calling for an artillery strike, they knew, would be useless. Almost all available Loyalist artillery was now in action elsewhere on the front since early estimates had indicated heavy guns would not be needed in this area. One air strike had been attempted, but all it had succeeded in doing was blowing the steeple off the church. Tanks were of little use, since they needed to be followed up by infantry, and the open areas on either side of the church made infantry attacks highly vulnerable.

Finally Major Merriman decided there was only one way to do the job, and that was by using small three- and five-man squads advancing on the church from all sides at staggered intervals. At dawn the next day the first of these small squads of infantry, armed with grenades and the ever-present firebombs made from bottles of gasoline—in World War II these came to be called Molotov cocktails—crept out toward the church. Leading one of these squads was Major Merriman.

As the squads approached the church, they were met by a storm of machine-gun and small-arms fire, but gradually a lone man here and a few there managed to make their way to the exterior walls of the church. There they took shelter beneath overhanging rock ledges at the bases of the walls, where they were inaccessible to Rebel arms fire. These men remained sheltered by the rock ledges all during the day, only occasionally being joined by other members of the Lincoln Brigade.

As darkness began to fall, the Lincolns stole from under the foundation ledges and began throwing their hand grenades and gasoline-bottle bombs through the church's window openings. This grenade attack was continued all night, and at dawn Major Merriman led the way with a dozen or so other Lincolns who stormed inside the building.

As Merriman and his men entered one end of the church, its defenders began to retreat out the other end. They defended their retreat with thrown grenades, rifle fire, and booby-trapped grenades. But within an hour the church was in the Lincoln Brigade's hands, and Merriman signaled for the rest of the Internationals to advance.

When these reinforcements arrived, they were disturbed to see that their commander, Major Merriman, was dripping blood from half a dozen wounds. Fortunately, these wounds proved to be only superficial ones from grenade fragments, and as soon as a medic had washed and patched up Merriman, he was ready to continue the fight.

During the next forty-eight hours the Rebel troops in the rest of Belchite began to surrender in droves. When they surrendered, many of them came forward shouting *"¡Viva la República! ¡Viva la República!"*

(Long Live the Republic of Spain), hoping this would gain them better treatment at the hands of the Loyalists. Franco's propagandists had led the Rebels to believe that if they were captured, they would be tortured and shot. When the XV International Brigade, led by the Americans in the Lincoln Brigade, began to share their meager food and water rations with the captured Rebels, not only did the prisoners respond gratefully, but some also offered to fight on the Loyalist side.

To rest up for the remainder of the campaign, the International Brigade was moved back to the peaceful town of Azaila just off the Belchite–Madrid Road. While they were in Azaila, they were visited by both Martha Gellhorn and Ernest Hemingway. The first man the two correspondents sought out was Major Merriman, and Gellhorn later cabled her magazine, *Collier's*, the following:

> *They said we could find Bob Merriman, the chief of staff, down there somewhere. We found him, and he took us to a lean-to, built of reeds, that rattled in the wind. He explained the offensive to us, drawing the plan of it on the dirt of the floor, going over every point carefully as if it were his freshman class in economics back in California.*
>
> *"The boys did well," Merriman said. There was dust on his glasses and he had very white*

*teeth. He was a big man, but shy and stiff, and his voice made you want to call him "Professor."*

*"This is a fine brigade we've got here," he said. "Shock troops, now. You can tell a brigade is fine when they move it from front to front, in trucks, fast, to wherever the danger is."*

Hemingway also wrote a news story about his interview with Merriman for the North American Newspaper Alliance. In it, however, he dealt mainly with the actual events of the Quinto-Belchite battles, although he too romanticized Merriman and the Lincoln Brigade in his lead. It read:

*When we got up with the Americans, they were lying under some olive trees along a little stream. The yellow dust of Aragon was blowing over them, over their blanketed machine guns, over their automatic rifles and their anti-aircraft guns. It grew in blinding clouds raised by the hoofs of pack animals and the wheels of motor transports, and in the gale of clouds of dust rolling over the bare hills Aragon looked like a blizzard in Montana.*

*But in the lee of the stream bank the men were slouching, fearful and grinning, their*

*teeth flashing white slits in their yellow pow-*
*dered station. Since I saw them last spring,*
*they have become soldiers.*

Shortly after he and his men settled down for their
rest in Azaila, Major Merriman sent a staff car and a
message back to his wife Marion in Albacete. The note
asked Marion to join him in Azaila, using as an excuse
the fact that the XV International Brigade's records
were in an awful state and needed to be straightened
out. Actually the records of the men killed and
wounded in the Quinto-Belchite battles did need to be
updated, but Merriman's desire to see his wife yet once
again perhaps was the greater need.

Once Marion arrived at Azaila, the Major and his
wife moved into a house in the small nearby village of
Almachuel. From here his troops were easily accessible
yet the couple also had some privacy. At first they both
were somewhat uneasy over the possible resentment
the men just returned from combat might feel about
their commander having the special privilege of a wife
waiting in the wings. But the troops made it perfectly
clear this was not the case. They were delighted to see
Marion, since many regarded her as something of a
mascot who brought them good luck. Because she
again managed to write letters for a good many of the
men to their sweethearts, wives, and families at home,
she was doubly welcome.

Early in her stay with her husband Marion was surprised to have him begin talking to her about her returning to the United States. The point of Merriman's argument was that she could actually do more good in the United States raising money for the Loyalists than she could do in Spain. Hemingway had still been optimistic about the Loyalist cause, but not quite as optimistic as he had been in the beginning. Both he and a *New York Times* correspondent, Herbert Matthews, had made it clear to Merriman what desperate financial straits the Loyalists in general and the Lincoln Brigade in particular were in. Money *must* be raised in the United States, and Major Merriman's wife seemed the logical person to head this fund-raising drive.

Marion postponed her decision, wanting to concentrate as much as possible just on being with her husband and trying to forget the war. This he would not let her do, however, insisting that she come with him to Belchite, where he could show her how that battle had gone.

Belchite, which was now held by a Loyalist occupying force, still reeked of the recent battle. Cordite fumes from exploding shells still filled the air, but overwhelming everything was the stench of dead bodies. The Fascist Rebels had made no effort to dispose of their dead, and now it was up to the Loyalists to dig mass graves and perform perfunctory burial services.

Merriman led his wife through the town, showing her just how the battle had taken place, from the church fortress to the various other strongpoints that the Lincolns had knocked out in the final house-to-house street fighting. When the grim tour was over, Marion was only too eager to return to their peaceful village.

Late in October the Loyalist high command decided to give up the proposed attempt to capture Saragossa. Shortly after the Belchite victory the Mac-Pap Battalion was sent against the Rebels at Fuentes de Ebro along the Ebro River. Fuentes de Ebro formed a protective shield that would need to be captured if Saragossa were to be attacked. In this effort the Lincolns were held in reserve, but they saw some action late in the fight.

The effort to capture Fuentes de Ebro failed, and on October 24 the Americans were relieved by a Spanish brigade. So the Aragon offensive came to an end with what Merriman and his men regarded as an only partial yet major success. The key towns of Quinto and Belchite had fallen, and most gratifying of all, during the Aragon fighting, out of more than 500 Americans engaged, just 23 men had been killed and 60 wounded.

Having gotten the records of the American casualties up to date, Marion returned to Albacete. Meanwhile, when the plan to attack Saragossa was abandoned in late October, the Lincoln Brigade, along with the rest of the XV International Brigade, was taken out of the combat area and sent to the rear. The men first spent a week in Quinto and then were sent farther to the rear at Ambite for reorganization and further training. This "further training" consisted mainly of getting acquainted with the new recruits who had undergone some training at Albacete and nearby Tarazona.

While this rest and recuperation was taking place, the XV International Brigade was formally incorporated into the Spanish army. Although this appeared to be nothing more than a technical action, it indicated to the veteran American combat men that the romantic period of their activity in the Spanish Civil War was over and a new period of grim professionalism had begun.

Meanwhile, at Albacete, Marion Merriman had helped organize a celebration for the first anniversary of the International Brigades in Spain. The celebration included a parade and festival and a rousing speech by La Pasionaria, who had come from Madrid just for the occasion.

Shortly after this celebration Major Merriman renewed his suggestion to Marion that she return to the United States and go on a fund-raising tour. Again Marion tried to postpone her decision, but now her husband was insistent. Finally, early in November, Marion agreed to make the trip. She also made a last-minute effort to get him to go with her, but his only response was a wordless shake of his head. Sadly they said good-bye for what was to be the last time.

Marion traveled by train to Paris, a train that was loaded with wounded Americans and British being sent home. In Paris she booked passage on the S.S. *Manhattan.* Late in December, after a week's passage across the Atlantic, Marion arrived in New York. There she was interviewed by both newspaper and radio reporters, and the fact that an American woman had actually served with the Spanish Loyalist army as a corporal in the Abraham Lincoln Brigade made headlines.

The first word she had from her husband was his report that he and his men had been taking part in a battle to capture the ancient walled city of Teruel.

# 10

▼▼

# WINTER FIGHTING
# AT TERUEL

Teruel was situated in the wintry hills east of Madrid. The Fascist Rebels had taken and consolidated this city earlier, planning eventually to advance from there to the Mediterranean and thus cut the Loyalist army in that area of Spain down the middle. To prevent this the Loyalist forces launched their attack at Teruel before the Rebels could begin their drive to the sea.

Edwin Rolfe has called Teruel "Spain's Valley Forge." After Teruel the Lincolns said: "Spain's the only place in the world where you can be up to your knees in hot sand one week and have snow blowing in your face the next." Even the Spanish admitted that winter brought to Teruel the worst weather to be found in Spain. The winter of 1937 was no exception.

For morale purposes the Spanish high command at first decided to hold the International Brigades out of the Teruel offensive. The Internationals had borne much of the brunt of the heavy fighting in the last campaign. In addition the capture of Teruel, a provincial capital of some 20,000 people, would be considered quite a prize to the Spanish people. It would be a morale booster to have the feat accomplished by Spanish troops.

Consequently, on the morning of December 15 the Spanish army of some 100,000 men with General Enrique Lister in command began the advance. To avoid warning the Rebels in Teruel of the attack, Lister ordered it to begin without preparatory aerial or artillery bombardment. Also a heavy snow was falling, which would mask the attack. Lister's plan was to surround the town, and by nightfall this had been accomplished. The next day the attack upon the city itself began.

For the next week there was continuous fighting within Teruel, and the Loyalists made slow but steady progress. This progress was misinterpreted outside the city, and on Christmas day Barcelona Radio falsely reported the Loyalists had captured Teruel. Actually there were still several thousand Rebels holding out inside key buildings at the center of the city, and Franco had not yet begun his all-out counterattack from outside the city walls. The Rebels within the city center did not, in fact, surrender until January 6. When they did so, Colonel Francisco Rey d'Harcourt, their commander, was branded a traitor by the Franco forces although Rey had held out long enough to enable the

Franco counterattack outside the city to get fully under way.

In the hills outside Teruel the battalions of the XV International Brigade got the false word of Teruel's capture. They were in several little towns where they had been moved on December 10 as reserve troops. As news of Teruel's apparent capture reached the men of the Lincoln Brigade, it seemed fitting that they were being visited by one of America's great singers and actors, Paul Robeson. Robeson helped the men celebrate Christmas by singing spirituals in the freezing open air. As his powerful voice went echoing among the winter hills and down the snow-choked valleys, it was later said men stopped in the midst of battle just to hear it.

Robeson was already a legendary black American. The son of a slave, he had gone on to become an early leader in the civil rights movement. A huge man with an equally huge voice and mind to match, he had attended Rutgers University. There he had been an all-American football player and a member of Phi Beta Kappa. After graduating from Rutgers he had gone to Columbia Law School, supporting himself by playing professional football. But once he received his law degree, Robeson saw little future for a black lawyer in race-conscious America. Consequently, he decided to become a professional actor and singer.

He was an almost immediate success on the stage,

starring in such Eugene O'Neill plays as *All God's Chillun Got Wings* and *The Emperor Jones.* Perhaps his most memorable musical effort up to this time had been in Jerome Kern and Oscar Hammerstein's *Show Boat*, in which his rendition of the song "Ol' Man River" became a classic.

Robeson went on to act in additional plays as well as motion pictures. At the invitation of Soviet film director Sergei Eisenstein, Robeson went to Russia in 1934 and was much impressed by the racial freedom he encountered there. From that time on he became a strong Soviet sympathizer and civil rights leader, although he always stoutly denied being a member of the Communist Party.

All during the thirties Robeson responded to any and all causes of the liberal left, and that was what brought him to Spain and the Abraham Lincoln Brigade. No entertainer of comparable stature had visited the Americans in Spain, and they and the Spanish people loved him, calling him affectionately "Pablo" and—despite his great size—"Pablito."

But the Americans' cause for celebration was relatively short-lived. Soon they received word that Teruel had not fallen, and on December 29 Franco unleashed his counterattack to relieve the city. The Internationals were not yet ordered into action, but they were put on the alert.

At this point one of the worst blizzards of the century struck the Teruel mountain area. Temperatures

94

fell to twenty degrees below zero, four feet of snow blocked all roads, and airplane flight was stopped by ceiling-zero conditions. The latter situation handicapped the Rebels more than the Loyalists because the Rebels had steadily been building up their air force with additional Heinkels from Germany and Fiats from Italy.

The Rebels and their German and Italian allies now had some 400 aircraft in the war, outnumbering the Loyalist planes—most of them Russian—by some two or three to one. As more and more Spanish cadet pilots, both Rebel and Loyalist trainees, were sent abroad to learn to fly, more and more new aircraft were turned over to them. Recently the Germans had also begun to supply the Spanish Rebels with squadrons of Messerschmitt 109 fighters that proved to be unbeatable in combat. The highly prized Me.109s, however, were flown only by members of the German Condor Legion. The Me.109 would also prove to be a formidable foe to British and American flyers in World War II.

But with each additional squadron of planes they sent—there were six planes in a squadron—both Mussolini in Italy and Hitler in Germany demanded more insistently that Franco show greater signs of ending the war in a hurry. Mussolini's son-in-law, Foreign Minister Count Galeazzo Ciano, expressed *Il Duce*'s discontent by writing in his diary, "His [Franco's] objective is always the ground, never the enemy. He just doesn't realize wars are won by destroying the enemy." Hitler's chief of staff, Field Marshal Wilhelm Keitel, spoke for the *Führer* when he said Franco seemed to welcome suggestions but then never carried them out.

But Franco was no fool. A short war, he told his aides, would end in negotiations. A long, cruel war was necessary for total victory, and total victory was his goal. He also reasoned, not inaccurately, that both Italy and Germany were now so far committed to Franco and his Nationalist Rebels that they couldn't back out no matter how many times they threatened to do so.

Nevertheless, despite the blizzard, despite subzero temperatures and fifty-mile-an-hour winds, Franco continued to send his all-out counterattack forward. Soon it was the Loyalists' turn to be besieged within the walls of Teruel. Outside the city this counteroffensive was extremely slow, since the cold froze all automotive vehicles to a virtual standstill. In addition Rebels and Loyalists alike suffered severely from frostbite, and the incidence of amputated frozen fingers and toes as well as arms and legs increased daily.

But inside the city, where doors and furniture could be burned to keep the inhabitants from freezing, the fighting was intense. Slowly the Loyalist lines were pushed back. As the Loyalists retreated inside the city, more and more requests went out for the Internationals to join the fighting. These requests were not honored until mid-January because the Internationals were rebuilding their forces.

Meanwhile, the skies began to clear, and as they did,

the Rebels were able to get their planes into the air and attack the hills surrounding the city. These aerial attacks were followed up by Rebel infantry, and soon several hilltops were back in Rebel hands. Once these heights were seized, the Loyalists inside Teruel began to be bombed by artillery from these hills as well as from Heinkel bombers.

Finally on January 16 the Internationals were flung into battle.

The British battalion of the XV International Brigade was the point unit in the final attempt to defend Teruel. British fighting men took up positions on three hilltops outside the city not yet taken over by the Rebels. Their units were connected only by field telephone, and their positions were further endangered by the snow, which made it virtually impossible to get food to them. Nevertheless, the British stopped an attempt by the Rebels to enter Teruel through a valley leading directly into the city.

The Rebel response to the spirited British defense was to unleash a fierce aerial bombardment. To prevent the XV Brigade's being driven out of the hills, the Mac-Pap Battalion was sent up in relief. At the same time, the Lincoln Brigade was sent on through the hills into the outskirts of Teruel itself near the city walls.

The Lincolns bivouacked in the tunnel of an abandoned railway. Outside the tunnel they dug defenses and emplaced their machine guns. Nearby, at the base of a city wall, there was a suburban town filled with deserted shops. During a lull before the infantry fighting began, the Lincolns found a clothing store that had been blown open by Rebel bombs. By this time many of the Lincolns' uniforms were so worn they were about to fall off, so some of the men began to reoutfit themselves in everything from top hats—their tin helmets didn't stop bullets anyway, they said—to tailcoats and pinstripe trousers. They also replaced their worn-out boots with patent leather shoes and fancy riding boots. They then returned to man their machine guns in what looked more like masquerade garb than it did combat gear.

Once the Rebel air and artillery barrage lifted for good, the British battalion, the Mac-Paps, and the Lincolns were attacked in frontal assault by the Rebel infantry. The British took heavy casualties, and the Mac-Paps were forced to retreat slowly from Teruel. The Lincolns held their ground until they gradually began to be outflanked on their left. To prevent being outflanked and eventually surrounded, the Lincolns also began to slowly retreat. They were harassed by steady small-arms and machine-gun fire and trench mortars. The men had come to hate and fear the trench mortars most, because their shells arrived silently and exploded with a vicious hail of steel slivers.

During this last-ditch attempt to retreat as slowly as possible, the Lincolns lost yet another commander, Philip Detro, a National Guardsman from Texas. Six feet four inches tall, Detro was an inviting target for snipers, and on January 19 a sniper's explosive bullet hit him as he was crossing between Lincoln entrenchments. He died several weeks later in the hospital at Murcia.

Actually the Lincolns managed to delay their retreat for some three weeks, but finally their casualties mounted to the point where they were ineffective as a unit. They were relieved by a Spanish Division called the Campesinos after their colorful commander, El Campesino (the Peasant). El Campesino (Valentín González) was a legendary figure who had been falsely reported killed so many times that he was regarded by his fiercely loyal men as having a charmed life.

The Lincolns were returned to rest camp in the Tajuna Valley via railroad transport. They had to ride in unheated box cars, but so elated were they about being out of battle that they sang along the way.

En route to the rest camp they were joined by Major Merriman, who told them that Commander Copič of the XV International Brigade was being sent on rest leave and that he, Merriman, was taking over as brigade commander. His announcement was greeted by cheers.

The men had not long either to cheer or to rest, however, for within a matter of days they were ordered back into battle to stem a Rebel drive that had broken the Loyalist lines beyond Teruel. Reluctantly the Lincolns and the rest of the XV Brigade returned to combat. But before the Internationals could make their presence felt, the Rebels had surrounded El Campesino and some 14,000 other Loyalist troops and threatened to annihilate them.

The Lincolns were instrumental in helping these surrounded men break out of the trap, but beyond that any additional offensive seemed out of the question. The Battle of Teruel, which had started out so favorably for the Loyalists, had ended in ignominious defeat.

Casualties on both sides were great, but the Rebels had clearly won the morale battle since they were the victors. Nevertheless, the Rebels suffered some 50,000 casualties—at least a third of them to the cold. Although they lost almost half of their air force and hundreds of pilots, more of these losses were from bad weather than enemy action. The Loyalist casualties were even higher, totaling more than 60,000 men and most of their air force.

Historian Peter Wyden has pointed out that the exhausted Loyalists in their retreat from Teruel were so hurried that they failed to notice the last-minute additions to the Rebel air force of the Condor Legion's first three combat-ready Junkers Ju.87 A-1 dive-bombers. These were the first of the infamous Stukas that were to terrorize the populace in the Germans' first *Blitzkrieg* advances into Polish, French, and other territory in World War II. The Stukas could dive at a seventy-degree angle as they hurtled downward to drop their bombs, and their dives were accompanied by a piercingly shrill whistle that added to the panic the dive-bombers created.

The loss of Teruel to the Rebels caused great dissension in the Spanish high command. La Pasionaria publicly attacked the conduct of the war up to this point. She was joined by others in her public protests, many of which reached the newspapers.

The rank and file of the Lincoln Brigade paid little attention to this political turmoil regarding the conduct of the war. But their commander, Major Merriman, was keenly aware of it and wrote his wife in the United States to that effect. She had been planning to return to Spain in March, but this now appeared to be unwise. The letter was one of the last Marion would receive from her husband, who was about to lead his men in what would come to be commonly called "The Retreats."

# 11

▼▼

## MISSING IN ACTION

The Lincoln Brigade, along with the other battalions in the XV International Brigade, was allowed to rest for a few days at Hijar at the end of February. There they nursed their wounds and tried to regain their strength from two months of winter warfare.

But early in March they were returned to the scene of an earlier triumph, Belchite. Theoretically the Lincolns were to continue their rest and recuperation there. The truth of the matter was that the Loyalists had learned Franco was planning a new attack in the Aragon region, and Belchite would probably be one of his early objectives.

In her public criticism of the Loyalist conduct of the war, La Pasionaria had pointed out that after its capture by the Loyalists, Belchite had never been refortified as a strong point in the Republic's defenses. A Spanish rifle regiment had simply been assigned to occupy the key city, but beyond that no attempt at building up the city's defenses had been made. La Pasionaria's words of warning were about to prove correct.

Now in command of the Lincoln Brigade was Dave Riess from Paterson, New Jersey. New Yorker Erick Parker was Riess' aide and battalion commissar. By March 9, when Franco's forces suddenly struck on a wide front in the Aragon area, the Lincoln Brigade had been reinforced by trainees from Albacete and Tarazona and now numbered 550 men.

Some 80,000 Rebels launched this new Aragon offensive on a front extending from Teruel to a point north of Belchite. They were supported by several hundred planes, the Rebel air force having been resupplied by Italy and Germany, and an equal number of Italian Fiat tanks. The Loyalists had only some sixty Soviet Ilyushin airplanes available to support about 40,000 readily available combat troops.

The Lincoln Brigade in Belchite was first aware that a Rebel breakthrough had occurred when Spanish Loyalist artillerymen came streaming back through the American positions. These fleeing artillerymen said that the Rebels had broken through the frontlines at a town called La Puebla de Alberton about twenty miles north of Belchite.

At brigade headquarters Major Merriman immediately ordered the Mac-Paps to Azuara, several miles west of Belchite, to protect the Lincolns' left flank. In Belchite the Americans were to be supported by a

British battalion, and a Spanish battalion would protect the right flank on the east. Later the British were told to strengthen the protection of the right flank.

The Americans chose not to defend Belchite within the town itself. It could be used as a fallback position. Instead, the Lincolns moved out several miles north of the city and established their lines there, using a deserted monastery as an anchor.

The Rebels moved down quickly from La Puebla de Alberton and were attacking the Lincolns before the British could get into their flanking position. Early in the attack a Rebel artillery shell or an aerial bomb scored a direct hit on the Lincoln Brigade's command post, killing both Commander Dave Riess and his commissar aide, Erick Parker. Five members of the headquarters staff were also severely wounded.

Learning of this disaster, Major Merriman ordered the Lincolns to fall back to the southeast beyond Belchite. They were relentlessly harassed by the advancing Rebels as they made this move. Although the retreating Lincolns tried twice to reestablish their defensive line, they were prevented from doing so by the persistent Rebels. As night fell on March 10, the Lincolns were given their line-of-march orders for further retreat. But these orders were confused, and the battalion split up and went marching off in two different directions.

Major Merriman led one of these sections southeast, toward the towns of Lécera and Albalate del Arzopispo.

The second section was led by one of Merriman's brigade aides, John Gates, straight east toward the town of Azaila. A platoon from Gates' section almost immediately encountered the enemy. Half of the members of this platoon were killed and the others captured.

When the battalion split up, orders also went out to the Mac-Paps in Azuara to retreat toward Lécera and Albalate. The Mac-Paps received these orders shortly after getting word that battalion headquarters had been blown up—only the word they received was that International Brigade headquarters had been hit. Rumors then swept through the Canadian-American battalion that Merriman had been killed.

As the Mac-Paps marched disconsolately southeast to join up with the remnants of the Lincoln Brigade at Lécera, they were startled on the early morning of March 12 to see a tall, bespectacled figure standing beside the road. In the dawn mists some of the men thought they were seeing the ghost of Major Merriman, but he soon proved to be real enough and was standing there to give them encouragement to march on to Albalate. So happy were the men to see Merriman that several of them rushed over and embraced him.

At Albalate, however, there were large forces of Rebels massed near the town, so the Lincolns—now joined by what was left of the XV International Brigade—moved on to Hijar. Of the 550 men who had made up the Lincoln Brigade when the Rebel advance began at Belchite a few days earlier, there were just 100 left. The entire XV International Brigade totaled only 500 men. The Lincolns were now commanded by six-feet-two-inches-tall Captain Milt Wolff, whom the Spanish called "El Lobo" and whom Hemingway later described as "gaunt and tall as Lincoln himself." Wolff's aide and commissar was John Gates, who had managed to escape the enemy ambush on the way to Azaila. He and what was left of his section had joined the Merriman group.

Wolff, Gates, and a hard-as-nails Greek from New York, Nick Pappas, who now headed the Lincoln's machine-gun section, led their handful of men in a bloody defensive stand at Hijar. But after two days they were forced to retreat once again, this time to Caspe, where they arrived on March 16. There they fought for three more days before being relieved by some fresh Spanish troops. A day's march brought them to the village of Corbera (near the border of the Spanish state of Catalonia), where they, along with the rest of the XV Brigade, were to rest, recuperate, and be reinforced.

While they were getting their brief respite from combat at Corbera, the Americans learned that the rest of Republican Spain had heard of the Rebel advances and the people were once again rallying to the Loyalist cause. The newspapers in Barcelona, Madrid, and Valencia printed giant headlines calling for resistance to the last man and woman, and La Pasionaria urged

Loyalist soldiers to fight to the death. She also repeated her defiant slogan, "It is better to die on your feet than live on your knees."

There was widespread response to these pleas. Over-age civilians flocked to the front to aid in rebuilding fortifications. Recruiting stations throughout the Republican region of Spain stepped up their recruiting programs. Up to now army recruits had been offered three pesetas (30¢) per day; now they were offered five (50¢). The fact that farmers still were earning only about one peseta (10¢) per day was an added incentive to join the military, but did little to increase sorely needed crops.

Training of volunteers at Albacete and Tarazona was also speeded up, and prematurely graduated trainees were rushed to the International Brigade units. All the men who had been on rest furloughs from the XV International Brigade, including Commander Copič, returned to the brigade to fight side by side with their comrades. Copič's return, of course, meant Major Merriman's resumption of his chief-of-staff role, but neither he nor his men saw much change in his duties.

After the Americans were driven out of Belchite, Franco's headquarters announced that the Abraham Lincoln Brigade had been totally destroyed. Franco had made this same announcement after Teruel, only to have the Lincolns rise to fight yet another day. They were to do so once again in the first week in April in the face of a new Rebel attack, this time at Gandesa, a central market town that controlled much of the surrounding area west of the Ebro River.

On March 30 the Lincolns received word that the Rebels were about to attack Gandesa. To blunt this attack the Lincolns, led by Captain Wolff, moved out to a road junction at the town of Batea. At the same time the Mac-Paps and the British battalion set up their defenses at the town of Calaceite. With the Spanish battalion in reserve the XV International Brigade thus formed a protective screen before Gandesa.

On April 1, beating the enemy to the punch, the Lincolns attacked the Rebels in the hills beyond Batea. Caught completely by surprise, the Rebels suffered severe losses. After their days and weeks of steady retreat, the Americans were elated at their ability to strike back successfully. That night they dug in at the crest of their newly occupied hills.

But the next morning Major Merriman drove up to the Lincoln positions in an armored car. He told the men they had to retreat to the fork in the Gandesa road at Batea, because the Rebels had overrun the town of Calaceite and were threatening to cut them off from the rear. If the Rebels succeeded in this maneuver, the Lincolns would be surrounded. Dutifully the Lincolns retreated from their hard-won hills while Major Merriman assumed command. Technically, of course, Milt Wolff was still commander of the battalion, but because of his senior rank Merriman assumed temporary control.

By April 3 the Lincolns had dug in in the hills above Gandesa. When they had begun their rearward march, they had discovered that there were already Rebel troops at Batea. Circling around these troops, they reached the outskirts of Gandesa—only to discover that Rebels had also begun to occupy that town. There were still Loyalist troops inside Gandesa, however, and the next move for the Lincolns seemed to be to break through the Rebels attacking the city and join the Loyalists inside it. Needless to say, with the steady deterioration of the Loyalist situation there was general confusion among the Lincolns as well as among the Mac-Paps and the British battalion, who were now fighting their way back from Calaceite. Corbera had already fallen to the Rebels, and it looked as if should Gandesa also fall, the entire Loyalist front along the Ebro River would collapse.

From their vantage point in the hills above Gandesa the Lincolns could now see more Rebel troops headed toward the town from Corbera. Despite the continually growing strength of the enemy, the Lincolns decided to try to break into the town and join their Loyalist comrades in their last-ditch defense. But they had barely launched their attack when the Rebels drove them off. Retreating once again to their positions in the hills, the Lincolns waited for nightfall, when they hoped to be able to escape by circling around Gandesa and heading for the Ebro River. Early that evening the Rebels sent one attack against the Lincolns, but this

110

was turned back by what was left of Nick Pappas' machine-gun section.

When darkness finally did fall, the men came out of the hills in single file and carefully made their way through the enemy positions. Later Captain Wolff said, "It would be useless to describe my feelings or the feelings of the men as we made our way through the dark in hostile, unknown territory. But this I believe: that there wasn't a man who made that trip who didn't feel death walking by his side."

In the middle of the night they approached enemy-occupied Corbera, which the Lincolns themselves had occupied a few days earlier. With greater caution than ever the remnants of the Lincolns crept through the enemy encampment. Leading one group of about thirty-five men were Major Merriman, the brigade commissar, Dave Doran, and Milt Wolff. As they moved silently in Indian file, they could hear the sleeping sounds of the Rebels around them—snoring, coughing, and restless stirring. A few whispered conversations of the Rebels who were supposed to be on guard duty could also be heard. Behind this advance party of Lincolns led by Merriman came a still larger body of men, perhaps 150, headed by Pappas' machine-gunners.

The next events occurred so quickly that none of the men involved could afterward recall exact details. What apparently happened is as follows: Suddenly the smaller group of Lincolns, headed by Merriman,

Doran, and Wolff, stumbled right into the middle of a company of wide-awake German and Spanish Rebel troops. This may have been an ambush. In any event, one of the Spanish Rebels immediately began to shout, *"¡Cabo de guardia, cabo de guardia!"* (Corporal of the guard, corporal of the guard!) This cry, of course, was to alert the Rebel guard mount that the enemy was in their midst. It is used universally by the military, including the U.S. army.

As soon as the cry went up, some of the Americans broke in one direction and some in another. Merriman and Doran, unfortunately, led a small group that headed directly toward the heart of the Rebel encampment. Moments later Wolff and the group of Lincolns fleeing in the opposite direction heard an order go up from the area to which Merriman and his group had fled, *"¡Manos arriba! ¡Manos arriba!"* (Hands up, hands up!) There then followed a series of shots. This was the last that any of the Lincoln Brigade ever knew of what happened to their commander.

Undoubtedly Merriman and Doran, and the men who were with them, were immediately shot. Their chances of being taken alive as prisoners were slim. Knowing this, they would probably have tried to shoot their way out. It was generally believed that all Loyalist officers were shot by the Rebels if captured, although enlisted men were usually taken prisoner. Occasionally, very occasionally, officers too were taken prisoner to be used for exchange purposes, but officers in the International Brigades would never be spared. Franco despised all foreign volunteers on the Loyalist side, although he obviously welcomed them among the Rebels. Franco also had a standing rule that no appeals for clemency should reach him until after the execution of the sentence.

If Merriman and his comrades were indeed shot, as seems most probable, none of their bodies were ever found by the Loyalists. The chances are that they and other dead Internationals were buried in a common unmarked grave by the Rebels.

The Lincolns who survived the sudden fatal encounter with the enemy did not, of course, linger in the area to see what had happened. They were too busy fleeing for their lives. Their destination was still the Ebro River east of Corbera, which, if they reached it and were able to swim across it, would offer them brief sanctuary in what was still Loyalist territory of the Spanish Republic.

# 12

## BEYOND THE EBRO

Only forty or fifty members of the Abraham Lincoln Brigade escaped across the Ebro River. The rest were either killed or captured during the retreats in Aragon. Once beyond the Ebro the men were relatively safe for the time being, since Franco aimed his next major attack not to the north against Barcelona, but to the south against Valencia.

One of the reasons Franco wanted to capture Valencia was that the seat of Republican government was now there. Early in the war, when it seemed possible that Madrid might fall, the Loyalists moved their government from the original capital to Barcelona. More recently, however, when Barcelona fell under heavy aerial bombardment and it appeared that *it* might fall, the seat of government was moved to Valencia. Capturing the city from which the Republic was currently being governed would not result in any financial gains for the Franco forces, since the Republic's gold reserves had much earlier been moved to Moscow. But there would be enormous gains in morale resulting from such a military success, which might just end the war.

Another reason Franco temporarily put off attacking Barcelona was that he feared such an attack might result in France's entering the war on the side of the Loyalists. Within recent weeks Barcelona had been bombed unmercifully from the air, culminating in the raids of March 19 to 21 when Rebel planes bombed the city every two hours for three days and two nights. This was the worst aerial bombing that any city had experienced since airplanes had begun being used in warfare (such bombings became commonplace in World War II), and as a result a great outcry arose throughout the western world against Franco's barbaric tactics. France had then begun to make open threats about entering the war in retaliation. The fact that Barcelona was relatively close to the French border as well as French ports on the Mediterranean also influenced French reaction. Since Franco definitely did not want war with France, he temporarily turned his attention away from Barcelona and centered it on Valencia.

The Lincolns now had their longest respite from combat since the early days of the war at Jarama. They put the time away from the front lines to good use. First of all they had to rebuild the battalion's manpower. Some of this buildup came, as usual, from trainees at Albacete and Tarazona—but only a small proportion. American volunteering had begun to slack off, so the battalion had to be brought up to strength with Spanish draftees. As a matter of fact by the time the Lincoln Brigade went back into battle, its membership was one-quarter Americans and three-quarters Spaniards.

The Spanish draftees were all young, ranging in age from fifteen or sixteen to their early twenties. All were extremely eager to learn, and all were enormously pleased to be serving with the Americans. Most of the Spanish youths were fans of American jazz music, and one lad in particular, Hilario, was determined to become "the Benny Goodman of Spain" after the war. Unfortunately, as Edwin Rolfe later wrote, the youngster did not survive the war. Nevertheless, while he was training with the Lincolns, Hilario kept them entertained with his jazz singing. He also managed to become the battalion bugler. "He was an artist with his horn," Rolfe said, "and often woke the men at dawn with 'Minnie the Moocher,' and sometimes at night he played 'Star Dust' instead of Taps."

The surviving Lincolns soon fell to with a will, training their young Spanish charges, and within a matter of weeks had a respectable infantry unit once again ready for action.

Among the last of the American volunteers to join the rebuilding Lincolns was twenty-three-year-old Jim Lardner. Lardner was the son of the famous American writer Ring Lardner, and until the spring of 1938 had been a reporter on the Paris edition of the *New York*

*Herald Tribune.* While on the paper Lardner had followed the Spanish Civil War closely. In March while on vacation Lardner journeyed for the first time down into Spain to see the war at first hand. Lardner's companions on this trip were Ernest Hemingway and another correspondent from the *New York Herald Tribune,* Vincent Sheean.

Lardner was an unlikely-looking volunteer for any kind of military organization. Tall, thin, wearing heavy horn-rimmed glasses, he was a graduate of Andover and Harvard and looked like a vacationing student. His shy manner made both Hemingway and Sheean wonder just how Lardner managed to get along in the rough-and-tumble newspaper business. Consequently, both men were startled when after a few days in Spain Lardner asked them how he could join the Abraham Lincoln Brigade.

Both Hemingway and Sheean did their best to talk Lardner out of any such rash action. It was late in the war, they pointed out, a war that the Loyalists now stood a very good chance of losing. Furthermore, he could probably do far more good writing about the Lincoln Brigade's exploits than he could as a totally untrained volunteer.

This argument went on for several days, and when he could get no assistance from either Hemingway or Sheean, young Lardner began making friends with various Spanish military officials. He impressed the military men with his knowledge of the war as well as his obvious dedication to the democratic ideals of the Loyalist side. They were probably most impressed, however, with the fact that Lardner was the son of a famous American writer, and his addition to the ranks could possibly aid the Loyalist cause abroad. Finally they agreed to accept Lardner's enlistment, but they had no intention of letting him get near combat. They assigned him to a replacement battalion far from the action and planned to keep him there for the rest of the war.

But young Lardner was determined to get into combat. After a few weeks he simply walked away from the replacement depot and made his way to where the Lincolns were stationed in the town of Mora la Nueva. Along the way Lardner stopped off in Madrid to visit with Sheean, get a bath in Sheean's hotel room, and round up a fancy new uniform. At Mora la Nueva, after a brief interview with Battalion Commander Milt Wolff, Lardner was placed in the battalion's third company.

Sheean visited Lardner several weeks later, mainly to bring him a new pair of glasses, since he had smashed his pair in training at Mora la Nueva. Sheean was genuinely surprised to see how well Lardner fit into the battalion. The rest of the men apparently had not been in the least put off by his shyness, and he had become a popular and important member of the organization. His new uniform had been traded to various other battalion members for their well-worn garments, and although he had not yet been in combat, he looked and acted very much the veteran. He also seemed extremely happy with his new role. Later Sheean learned that by the time the Lincolns went back into action, Lardner had been promoted to corporal.

At about this time there began to be general talk about the removal of all foreign volunteers from the Loyalist forces. Such a move on the part of the Republican authorities would be something of a gamble. However, there was little doubt that the war was going badly for the Loyalists, and one of the reasons it was going badly was because of the huge numbers of Italian and German troops and the large amount of Italian and German equipment—tanks and planes and artillery—being supplied to the Rebels.

The Loyalist authorities hoped that if they withdrew all foreign volunteers from their ranks, pressure from abroad through the League of Nations—forerunner of the United Nations—would force Franco to cut off the foreign aid he was receiving for the Rebels. This was obviously a fairly farfetched gamble, but it was seriously being weighed by the Loyalist high command. For the time being, however, the plan was not put into effect, and the Lincolns as well as the other Internationals continued their preparation for one more major battle.

According to historian Hugh Thomas, the number of Germans serving in Spain with the Rebels reached a maximum of 10,000 men. Of these, some 6,000 served in the Condor Legion. Italian peak strength with the Rebels reached 50,000.

Helping the Loyalists, according to Thomas, were five International Brigades with a peak total of some 18,000 men. Although they came from more than 50 nations, most came from France, Germany and Austria, Italy, the United States, Great Britain, the Soviet Union, Canada, Yugoslavia, Hungary, and the Scandinavian countries. Although the Russians frequently seemed to predominate in the International Brigades, the number of men sent to Spain from the Soviet Union all through the war totaled fewer than 2,000 men and probably never exceeded more than 500 men at one time. Many of the volunteers from other countries, however, were members of the Communist Party, which was why the Internationals were usually called *"Rojos"* (Reds) by the Rebels. In addition, many of the military volunteers from the Soviet Union served in important positions in the International Brigades—on the general staff, etc.—which added to their Russian atmosphere.

The Lincolns—now 700 men strong, the largest the battalion had ever been—along with the rest of the XV International Brigade, went back into action late in July of 1938. Of these 700 men 200 were American. There were also about 50 or 60 Americans in the Mac-Paps and perhaps a dozen in the British and Spanish battalions. Their immediate task was to recross the

Ebro and then head for the scenes of their former triumphs and defeats at Corbera and Gandesa.

The recrossing of the Ebro was relatively simple, mainly because Franco had almost his entire air force as well as his artillery concentrated in the Valencia area. The crossing was made by the Lincolns using a portable pontoon bridge as well as small boats, which had been made available during the battalion's several months' rest. A few of the men waded and swam across the river with their rifles and other valuables strapped to their backs. Once on the opposite shore the Lincolns, still headed by the indomitable Captain Milt Wolff, moved rapidly inland toward the Rebel front lines.

This inland advance by all the Internationals lasted for several days. Then it began to slow down in the face of heavily concentrated Rebel fire. The Lincolns did not stop until they had once again reached the hills surrounding Gandesa. There they dug in and refused to be budged even by the most resolute of Rebel counterattacks.

Among those wounded in early August was Corporal Jim Lardner. Although it was only a slight wound—a piece of shrapnel in the thigh—he was kept out of action for several weeks. When he returned to the Lincolns, the Rebels had launched a strong counterattack, but they were not gaining much ground. Also upon his return he brought with him renewed rumors about the withdrawal of the International Brigades from the war. It was said that the League of Nations was now appointing a commission to repatriate all foreign nationals from Spain to their own countries. The men at the front had heard these rumors too but were too busy defending themselves to pay much attention to them.

The Lincolns were now occupying a key hill in an advanced position. The Mac-Paps and the Spanish battalion covered the Lincolns' flanks, and the British were a few hundred yards in the rear in reserve. The main problem with the Lincolns' position was that it was lower than that of the enemy on a high ridge to the southwest. From this ridge the Rebels poured down a steady barrage of artillery fire.

From the end of August through much of the month of September the Lincolns withstood this fire as well as frequent infantry attacks when the Rebel barrage lifted. Although they continued to lose men at a slow but steady rate, the Lincolns refused to give ground. Occasionally they were relieved by the British battalion, but as soon as the alert was sounded for a Rebel attack, the Lincolns were back in their frontline positions.

During this period Corporal Jim Lardner had to go back across the Ebro yet again, this time to have an infected tooth removed. He returned to the battalion September 22, bringing with him the morning's newspapers from Barcelona announcing that the League of Nations had stated that all foreign volunteers fighting

123

for the Loyalists were to be immediately withdrawn and repatriated to their own countries. No mention was made of Rebel volunteers. This sort of mindless inconsistency was one reason the League was ignored by most nations.

Despite this announcement plans proceeded for a Lincoln Brigade attack that night against the Rebel front line. Lardner rejoined his unit and prepared to take part in the attack, which went forward as soon as darkness fell. At one point Corporal Lardner was ordered to lead a patrol of several men to contact the Spanish battalion on the Lincolns' flank. One of the men in his patrol was an American private, Tony Nowakowsky. Several hours after the patrol went out, Nowakowsky returned, alone.

Nowakowsky reported that they had not made contact with the Spanish battalion but had run into what they thought was a Rebel frontline listening post. Lardner told the men in his patrol to stay right where they were while he went ahead to see who was in the outpost, if that was what it was.

Shortly after Lardner left the patrol, Nowakowsky said, he and the others heard some shouts and then a series of rifle shots and several grenade explosions. Almost immediately Nowakowsky and the rest of the patrol were also attacked, and Nowakowsky was the only one to escape unharmed.

That was the last anyone heard or saw of Corporal Jim Lardner. One of the last volunteers to join the

Lincoln Brigade, he was also one of the last to die. Soon afterward Vincent Sheean learned that Lardner was missing and filed a story stating that fact to his newspaper. Somewhat later Sheean incorporated the story in a book of reminiscences, *Not Peace but a Sword*, under the chapter heading "The Last Volunteer." For a brief period Lardner's loss was as widely talked about in the United States as the loss of Major Robert Merriman had been.

The next day, September 23, the Lincolns were driven off the hill they had been occupying, and they had no chance to further investigate Lardner's fate. There was little doubt, however, that he, like Major Merriman, had been shot and killed.

The night of the 23rd of September the Lincolns were relieved, once again by their Spanish friends the Campesinos. The Lincolns, along with the rest of the Internationals, were not merely being withdrawn from this battle. They were being withdrawn from the war.

It took more than a month to gather all the Internationals together. Then in late October there was a farewell parade at Albacete. But the most elaborate farewell affair took place in Barcelona in mid-November. There a huge parade and demonstration were held in the Internationals' honor. The parade route was strewn with flowers, and the Spanish people stood along the parade route and cheered their foreign volunteer friends until they were hoarse. Occasionally a young girl would dart out from the crowd and kiss one of the Internationals and then insist on marching beside him in the parade.

After the parade, at the reviewing stand, a number of officials made speeches. The most memorable speech, according to many of the remaining Lincoln Brigade members, was made by La Pasionaria. She said:

> *Mothers! Women! When the years pass by and the wounds of war are stanched; when the cloudy memory of the sorrowful, bloody days returns in a present of freedom, love and well-being; when the feelings of rancor are dying away and when pride in a free country is felt equally by all Spaniards—then speak to your children. Tell them of the International Brigades. Tell them how, coming over seas and mountains, crossing frontiers bristling with bayonets, and watched for by ravening dogs thirsty to tear at their flesh, these men reached our country as Crusaders for freedom. They gave up everything, their homes, their country, home and fortune—fathers, mothers, wives, brothers, sisters and children, and they came and told us: "We are here, your cause, Spain's cause, is ours. It is the cause of all advanced and progressive mankind." Today they are going away. Many of them, thousands of them, are staying here with the Spanish earth*

126

*for their shroud, and all Spaniards remember them with the deepest feeling.*

*Comrades of the International Brigades! Political reasons, reasons of State, the welfare of that same cause for which you offered your blood with boundless generosity, are sending you back, some of you to your own countries and others to forced exile. You can go proudly. You are history. You are legend. You are the heroic example of democracy's solidarity and universality. We shall not forget you, and when the olive tree of peace puts forth its leaves again, mingled with the laurels of the Spanish Republic's victory—come back!*

Immediately after La Pasionaria's passionate farewell the International Brigades began to make their way out of Spain and to their homes. The survivors of the Abraham Lincoln Brigade made their way to Paris by train. The Spanish Republic paid their way out of Spain, but the men had to pay their own steamship fares to the United States. Most of the men had back pay at their disposal, and those who did not either borrowed money from their buddies or obtained it from the Young Communist League headquarters in Paris.

Some of the men booked their return passage in groups of two and three. But most of the remainder decided to travel in one large group. By a curious coincidence this group of more than 100 men returned to the United States aboard the very same ship, the S.S. *Normandie*, that had brought the first Abraham Lincoln Brigade volunteers to France on the first leg of their journey into Spain back in December of 1936, almost exactly two years earlier.

Caves and trenches defended by the Loyalists outside of Brunete.

*Above:* Captain Milton Wolff (left) with Ernest Hemingway near the front lines.

*Opposite, top:* Robert Hale Merriman and members of the Lincoln Brigade in Quinto.

*Opposite, bottom:* Loyalist pilots take a break beside one of their Soviet-made fighter planes.

James Phillips Lardner.

Some of the survivors of the Lincoln Brigade who have returned, via steamship, to New York.

# AFTERWORD

The Civil War in Spain went on for several months
after the Lincolns and other Internationals were withdrawn from the Loyalist ranks. No foreign nationals
were ever withdrawn from the Rebel side, which soon
overwhelmed the Loyalists and won the war. The war
ended on March 28, 1939, and Franco became the
nation's dictator. Actually he was named *El Caudillo*,
or leader of the nation.

As had been widely predicted, World War II started
in September, just a few months after the end of the
Spanish Civil War. Interestingly, however, Spain did
not enter World War II. Both Hitler and Mussolini
expected Franco to bring his country into the conflict
on their side, but he refused to do so. "All our aid to
Franco," Hitler said, "was an absolute gift."

Finally Hitler arranged to meet with Franco at Hen-
daye, France, in 1940 to try and talk him into becoming an active ally of the Axis Powers, as Germany, Italy,

and Japan were called. But Franco outtalked the usually persuasive Hitler and turned him down. As a matter of fact Franco talked so much during the meeting that the *Führer* came away shaking his head and saying he would rather have several teeth pulled than to go through an experience like that again.

Somewhat later Franco relaxed his stand to the point where he furnished Germany with several submarine bases and allowed the crack "Blue Division" of Spanish infantry volunteers to fight side by side with the Germans against Russia. The Blue Division numbered about 50,000 men. There was no doubt about it—Franco did not like the Russians.

But officially Franco's Spain remained neutral all during World War II, although it continued to openly sympathize with the Axis. Interestingly, the young Americans who crossed the Pyrenees to get into Spain to fight with the Lincoln Brigade were not the last Americans to make that strenuous journey. During World War II many young American flyers based in England who were shot down over France and survived were picked up by the French underground fighters and spirited down across France to the Spanish border. From there they were on their own to climb the Pyrenees and escape into "neutral" Spain. In Spain they were usually temporarily jailed by the Spanish authorities and then released to the American Ambassador's staff, who saw to it that the escapees, as they were called, got back to England. Rumors during the war said that each of these flyers had to be ransomed at $10,000 per head in gold, but these rumors have never been proved or disproved.

As soon as Franco took over as dictator in Spain, thousands of Loyalists fled the country to avoid execution. Among the best known of these refugees was La Pasionaria, who fled to the Soviet Union, where she was made welcome. La Pasionaria lived in Russia for some thirty-six years—until Franco's death on November 20, 1975. Then she returned to Spain, where she lived on into the late 1980s, at which time she was over ninety years old. In a newspaper poll for "greatest living woman," reported in the European press in late 1975, there was a tie for first place between Israel's former prime minister, Golda Meir, and Dolores Ibarruri, La Pasionaria.

During the Civil War there were also many other Spanish refugees, most of them children. Following the bombing of Guernica in the spring of 1937, when hundreds of civilians were killed, parents in many towns and cities in northern Spain decided to evacuate their children. (Many Londoners took similar action when Germany began to bomb that city in World War II.) Thousands of Spanish children between the ages of two and fifteen were sent to sympathetic European countries. France and the Scandinavian countries accepted several thousand children.

About 5,000 Spanish refugees fled to the Soviet Union during the Civil War—about 4,000 children and 1,000 adults. Special schools for the Spanish *niños* (children) were set up in Russia, and books were printed to provide the children with an education in Spanish. Even teachers were brought from Spain.

In 1957 about 1,500 of these *niños* in Russia returned to Spain in a widely publicized "pardon" by Franco. Although the Spanish government promised jobs and housing for these returnees, many were disappointed with life in Spain, and some 10 percent emigrated to the Soviet Union for a second time.

After Franco's death several hundred *niños* drifted back into their native country. They found a much more democratic nation than Spain had been under *El Caudillo*'s regime. Former Prince Juan Carlos had become king. King Juan Carlos had promptly set about dissolving the country's Fascist government. Free elections were held in June of 1977, and moderates and Democratic Socialists became the largest parties. The Communist Party was also no longer outlawed, but it was not especially popular. In the two-house Parliament there were only 32 Communists out of a total of 598 members. The majority were Democrats.

By 1980 Catalonia and the Basque country were granted home rule, but both regions were still seeking total independence. This struggle continued in the late 1980s, with Spain a self-declared socialist society headed by a monarch. There continued to be much unrest in the country, most of it due to large-scale unemployment, which ran as high as 16 to 20 percent.

Tourism was one of Spain's leading industries both during Franco's postwar regime and after his death. The scars of the Civil War were virtually no longer visible by the 1980s, but one of the biggest tourist attractions was a huge mausoleumlike monument that Franco had erected to the oft-cited "one million" war dead in the "Valley of the Fallen" not far from Madrid.

Marion Merriman, Lincoln Brigade commander Robert Merriman's widow, did not return to Spain until 1979, when she was 70. Immediately after learning that her husband was missing in action during the war, she made every possible effort through U.S. State Department officials, Spanish government officials, friends she had made in Spain, journalists, and writers—including Ernest Hemingway—to find out what had happened to him. At first there were several heart-stopping rumors that Major Merriman was still alive. When these proved false, Marion gradually came to accept the fact that Bob was not coming back. But she could not bring herself to return to Spain, or to write of her and her husband's experiences there.

Eventually she remarried. Her second husband was Emil Wachtel, an attorney and businessman. Together Marion and Emil Wachtel raised three sons in Palo Alto, California. Marion remained active in an administrative job at Stanford University, and later was in charge of the San Francisco Bay Area Post of the Veterans of the Abraham Lincoln Brigade.

When her second husband died, Marion Merriman

Wachtel did finally return to Spain—more than forty years after Bob had been lost there. She could not, of course, find Bob's grave, but she did, she said, feel a sense of communion with him. She said this in a book she wrote with Pulitzer Prize journalist Warren Lerude, *American Commander in Spain: Robert Hale Merriman and the Abraham Lincoln Brigade*, which was published in 1986.

Another factor that kept Marion from writing such a book earlier was that right after the end of the Spanish Civil War and for many years thereafter the Abraham Lincoln Brigade was branded as a Communist—and thus un-American—organization. Although Bob Merriman and many other members of the Abraham Lincoln Brigade had not been card-carrying Communist Party members, all Brigade members became suspect in the public mind.

Most Americans did not trust Communists because they believed that all of them took their orders directly from leaders in the Soviet Union who were trying to force their form of government upon every country in the world. Suspicions of the Soviet Union's totalitarian intentions were strengthened when in August of 1939, just a month before the start of World War II, Russia signed a nonaggression pact with Germany. By signing this pact the Soviet Union agreed to remain neutral if Germany went to war to fulfill its own totalitarian ambitions. This gave Germany a free hand to attack

France and Great Britain in the west without having to fear an attack by Russia from the east.

Russia and Germany remained World War II allies until June of 1941. Then Germany suddenly turned on its Soviet ally and invaded Russia in an effort to conquer the whole of continental Europe. Immediately, Great Britain's Prime Minister Winston Churchill announced that the Soviet Union and Britain were now allies. The United States was not yet in the war; nevertheless it announced that it would begin sending military aid to Russia. Six months later, after the Japanese attack on Pearl Harbor on December 7, 1941, the United States entered the war and also became a staunch ally of Communist Russia.

However, despite the fact that the U.S. was now Russia's wartime ally, the American military establishment did not trust any Communists, or suspected Communists, within its ranks. It feared they would be subversive, or more loyal to Russia than to the United States. Consequently, during World War II veterans of the Abraham Lincoln Brigade were forced to undergo careful scrutiny before being accepted into the U.S. armed services, and it was frowned upon to send them overseas. Nevertheless, several hundred ex-Lincolns did serve overseas, and a number of them were decorated. The Abraham Lincoln Brigade, however, was one of a dozen or more organizations whose members were listed in "confidential" notices to all military intelligence organizations. The notices barred members from access to classified military reports of any kind.

The Lincoln Brigade veterans were disqualified from seeing such classified material because, the U.S. military high command declared, they were "PAF" or "Premature Anti-Fascists," and as such were considered suspect. Thus, the U.S. decreed, it was all well and good to fight against Fascism and totalitarianism, as millions of men were doing in World War II, but it had been a mistake to fight Fascism "prematurely" as the relative handful of Lincoln Brigade members had done in the Spanish Civil War.

What the U.S. military leaders and other critics ignored was the fact that the members of the Abraham Lincoln Brigade, Communists or non-Communists, were idealistic young Americans willing to fight and even die for the principles of freedom and democracy. In fact, some 900 Lincoln Brigaders lost their lives in Spain. In this they were no different from the young Americans who have fought for these same principles from the days of the American Revolution right down to the present.

Occasionally it has been asked, "What kind of government would Spain have had if the Loyalists had won the war?"

This is somewhat like speculating about what would have happened to Germany and Europe if Adolf Hitler had never been born. No one, of course, can possibly

140

answer such a question, and it is perhaps pointless to speculate about it.

The question about Spain, though, is more legitimate because some have suggested that if Franco had lost the Spanish Civil War, a Communist dictatorship would have resulted. But this is highly unlikely. First of all, the Communists were never that powerful or large enough in number to take over the government. They were, however, highly visible, which seemed to make them more powerful than they actually were.

As previously noted, among the international volunteers who actually fought on the Loyalist side, there were probably no more than a *total* of 2,000 Russians. Historian Hugh Thomas estimates there were fewer than this. Thomas also says there probably were never more than 500 at one time. The Russians did manage to serve in key roles—on the general command staff and in command of various training bases, including the Republican airfields. This made them much more conspicuous than the more numerous volunteers from other countries.

In addition on the Loyalist side, there were several thousand foreign volunteers plus several thousand Spanish soldiers who were converts to Communism. No one knows exactly how many such converts there were, but here again they were vastly outnumbered by those of other political persuasions—democrats, anarchists, socialists, Basque nationalists, etc., etc. It was only by combining all these widely disparate groups under the heading of the Popular Front that the war could be conducted at all, and there would have to have been a similar meeting of the minds in order to establish *any* kind of government, let alone a Communist government, if the Loyalists had beaten Franco. In fact it was something of a Popular Front that came to the fore following Franco's death and that governs Spain today.

Among the civilian population the Communists, again, were highly visible—typified by the colorful and flamboyant La Pasionaria—but by no means large enough in number to take over the government. At the start of the war in 1936 the Spanish Communists claimed a party membership of 35,000. Actually, again according to Hugh Thomas, there were probably only 10,000 Communist Party members at this time, as compared with, for example, a Socialist Party membership of 1½ million. Most of the other political parties also outnumbered the Communists, but not by so large a margin.

During the Civil War, at about the time of the siege of Madrid, Communist Party membership increased dramatically to perhaps 300,000. They were still outnumbered badly, however, by the Socialists, as well as by the Anarchists, who numbered over half a million. At this time the Communists tried to increase their strength by combining their forces with the Anarchists, but the Anarchists would have no part of such an alliance. By the war's end Communist Party membership had decreased to below its present levels, which are indicated by Communist representatives in the Parliament (see page 136).

At the time of Franco's death Communist leader Santiago Carillo hoped for a revival of his party when it was again declared a legal organization. But the longing of the Spanish people, especially the country's new middle class, for a change from dictatorship as well as for peace played a major role in the smooth transition to a constitutional monarchy similar to that of Great Britain.

"Spain is now a much better country to live in than it ever was," King Juan Carlos recently declared. "As a member of NATO [North Atlantic Treaty Organization], it is also for the first time in two centuries a solid piece of the Western world."

There are two final reasons the Spanish government probably could never have become a Communist dictatorship. First, Spain is essentially a Catholic nation—Roman Catholicism is the official state religion—and Communists are (officially) atheists. Karl Marx and Nikolai Lenin, founders of Soviet Communism, could not replace God in the minds of most Spanish people. Nor could the Communist "bible," the *Communist Manifesto*, replace the Christian Bible for most Spaniards.

Secondly, and perhaps most important of all, the Spanish people are traditionally highly independent and have a profound belief in the democratic way of life and in personal freedom. There are some medieval historians, in fact, who claim that the earliest forms of political democracy had their beginnings in Spain. Whether or not this is true, it is true that the Spanish people are freedom loving and instinctively opposed to most of the dictatorial aspects of Communism. It is true they bore up under the dictatorship of Franco, but they did this because they were physically forced to do so. Given a freedom of choice, as they had after Franco's death, or would have had earlier had Franco been defeated by the Loyalists, it is highly unlikely that they would have voted for a Communist government or allowed one to control their country.

# FURTHER READING

For many years I have collected books about the Spanish Civil War. Among the best books for young (or old) readers on this subject are, in my opinion, Edwin Rolfe's *The Lincoln Battalion*, first published by the Veterans of the Abraham Lincoln Brigade, New York, 1939, and *American Commander in Spain* by Marion Merriman and Warren Lerude, published by the University of Nevada Press, Reno, Nev., 1986. Unfortunately the former is long out of print and is available only in some libraries and through rare book dealers. Both books are clear, simply written, informative, and highly readable. The Rolfe book should be brought back into print.

One of Rolfe's fellow veterans of the fighting in Spain, Alvah Bessie, also wrote a book about his experiences there. It is *Men in Battle*, also published by the Veterans of the Abraham Lincoln Brigade, New York, 1939, 1954. The Bessie book, however, deals mainly with the latter months of the Lincoln Brigade's experiences, and is not as highly readable as Rolfe's book. It too is long out of print, but many libraries have copies of it.

Every writer, including this one, who has written anything on the Spanish Civil War is indebted to historian Hugh Thomas. His *The Spanish Civil War*, New York: Harper & Row, Publishers, was first published in 1961 and was thoroughly revised and updated in 1977. It is unquestionably the definitive book on the war and, so far as I have been able to determine, misses no important wartime fact or detail, large or small. But I would hesitate to recommend the Thomas book to a young reader, except an extremely advanced one, because it is so highly detailed.

Frequently one can get as much atmosphere and almost as much factual information in reading fiction about an event as in reading nonfiction about it. Consequently, I think Ernest Hemingway's novel *For Whom the Bell Tolls*, New York: Charles Scribner's Sons, 1940, is a must for anyone interested in the war. When I was in Spain touring the battle sites there, our guide said he assumed I was a Hemingway fan. I said I was. "All Americans are," he said. Then he said, "Let me recommend a couple of books by a Spanish author that are not so romantic as Hemingway's but are much nearer the truth as far as the Spanish Civil War goes." He did so, and when I was able to obtain them I found them to be fascinating novels that tell about the war

146

from both sides rather than just one, as most American and British novelists have done. They have been excellently translated into English and have been published in the United States. Their author is José Maria Gironella. I recommend them for advanced young readers. Their titles are *The Cypresses Believe in God*, New York: Alfred A. Knopf, 1958, and *One Million Dead*, New York: Doubleday, 1963.

The United States was not the only nation to lose gifted young men fighting for the Loyalists. The British lost several, including a young poet, John Cornford, who was the first Englishman to go to the front in Spain. He was killed there on the Cordoba front in late December 1936 on his twenty-first birthday. A history student at Trinity College, Cambridge, Cornford was the great-grandson of Charles Darwin. His poems and letters were published in paperback by the British publishers Carcanet Press Limited, 1986, under the title *John Cornford: Collected Writings*. The book is available through any good bookstore and is an emotionally moving and inspirational reading experience. British ex-members of the International Brigades, incidentally, were not ostracized as were so many Americans. Prime Minister Winston Churchill, for example, always referred to the British volunteers in Spain as "armed tourists."

Two other paperbacks are well worth obtaining. One is *The International Brigades: Spain—1936–1939* by Vincent Brome, 1965, first published in Great Britain by William Heinemann and later published by William Morrow in New York. The second is *The Civil War in Spain: History in the Making—1936–1939*, edited by Robert Payne, 1962, and published in New York, by Fawcett World Library (paperback) and G. P. Putnam's Sons (hardcover). This is an excellent collection of eye-witness accounts of the war by such writers as John Dos Passos, Arthur Koestler, André Malraux, George Orwell, and Eliot Paul.

Almost purely as a matter of interest I would like to suggest two books that young readers may encounter in libraries or in the collections of rare book dealers but are not apt to find elsewhere. These were published during the war and consequently have a unique flavor that postwar books do not have. The first is *The Spanish Cockpit*, by Franz Borkenau, which was first published in 1937 by Faber and Faber Ltd. in London. A journalist, Borkenau covered the early battles in close-up fashion as no other journalist, before or afterward, did. The second book is the photographer Robert Capa's *Death in the Making.* Capa too was a high-risk journalist who would virtually go anywhere and do anything to get war pictures. Born and brought up in Hungary, he took pictures all over the world and later became a special photographer for *Life* magazine in the United States. He was killed when he stepped on a land mine in Vietnam during the war there. *Death in the Making*, published by Covici, Friede, in New York in 1938, is filled with Capa's Spanish Civil War pictures as well as several by a French photographer, Gerda Taro, who was every bit Capa's equal in daring and almost his equal as a photographer. She died when she was crushed by a tank in a Spanish Rebel counterattack. Together she and Capa left a memorial of Spanish Civil War pictures that have not been surpassed by any other photographers in any other war for their honest depiction of war's grim horror. Capa's photograph of a Spanish infantryman taken just at the moment the infantryman has been mortally struck by a bullet is one of the most remarkable combat photographs ever made. It is on the jacket of *Death in the Making* and is also included in this book.

Below are several other books that young readers should find interesting and informative:

Beevor, Antony. *The Spanish Civil War.* New York: Peter Bedrick Books, 1982. Distributed in the United States by Harper & Row, New York.

Orwell, George. *Homage to Catalonia.* New York: Harcourt, 1952.

Paul, Eliot. *The Life and Death of a Spanish Town.* New York: Random House, Inc., 1937, 1942.

Sheean, Vincent. *Not Peace but a Sword.* New York: Doubleday, 1939.

Wyden, Peter. *The Passionate War.* New York: Simon and Schuster, 1983.

—D.L.

# INDEX

*Numbers in* italics *refer to photographs.*

# Index

# Index

# Index

# Index